C000257736

KS1 English
Comprehension

Teacher Book

This Teacher Book accompanies CGP's KS1 Targeted Comprehension Question Books for Year 1, Year 2 and Year 3 Ready.

It's packed with ideas for extra activities, progress charts and — of course — full answers to every question!

It's the perfect resource for planning and organising Comprehension sessions throughout KS1.

Contents

Year 1

Year 2

Year 3 Ready

When using the extra activities in this product, please take the safety of the participants into consideration at all times, and ensure that children are supervised when researching material for this product online. Teachers should also take into account pupils' personal circumstances when dealing with topics of a sensitive nature.

Published by CGP

Editors: Zoe Fenwick, Catherine Heygate, Holly Robinson
Consultants: Stephanie Lake, Maxine Petrie
Proofreaders: Janet Berkeley, Jill Cousner, Juliette Green,
Catherine Heygate, Anne James, Lucy Towle, Karen Wells

With thanks to Ana Pungartnik for the copyright research.

ISBN: 978 1 78294 761 5
Printed by Elanders Ltd, Newcastle upon Tyne.
Year 1 cover illustrated by Maa Illustrations. www.maaillustrations.com
Year 3 Ready cover image iStock.com/duncan1890

Text, design, layout and original illustrations © Coordination Group Publications Ltd. (CGP) 2017
All rights reserved.

Photocopying more than one chapter of this book is not permitted. Extra copies are available from CGP.
0800 1712 712 • www.cgpbooks.co.uk

Key Stage One Reading Comprehension

In this introduction, you'll find everything you need to help you get the most out of CGP's Key Stage One Targeted Comprehension range.

Reading comprehension is a key part of the National Curriculum

The English Programme of Study for the Key Stage One National Curriculum requires pupils to explore a variety of stories, poems and non-fiction texts. Pupils are expected to:

- develop fundamental reading comprehension skills;

- improve the accuracy and fluency with which they read;

- expand their vocabulary;

- develop pleasure in reading and a strong motivation to read.

CGP's Key Stage One Targeted Comprehension range

- CGP's Key Stage One Targeted Comprehension range is designed to introduce pupils to comprehension, and to support the development of their comprehension skills throughout Years 1 and 2. It is ideal for use in Guided Reading sessions.

- The range is packed full of engaging comprehension activities that gradually progress in difficulty. It begins with image-based activities at the start of the Year 1 book, before progressing to more traditional comprehension exercises based around texts of increasing length and complexity.

- There are three Targeted Question Books (see pages 2-4 for more information)...

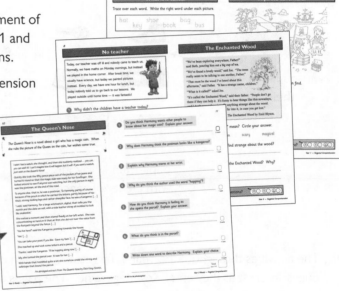

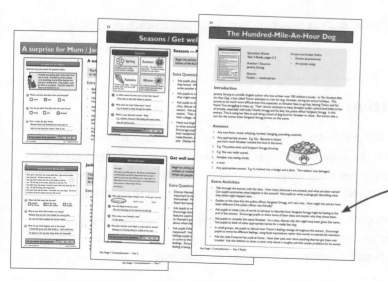

- ...and an accompanying Teacher Book. The range can be used in Guided Reading sessions, or as the foundation for a variety of other literacy lessons and activities.

- The extra activities in the Teacher Book have been designed to reinforce the Key Stage One curriculum — with a focus on literacy-based activities.

- Pupil progress charts make it easy to record and track pupils' performance.

The Targeted Question Books

The Key Stage One Targeted Comprehension range includes three Targeted Question Books. With separate books for Year 1 and Year 2, and a Year 3 Ready book designed to bridge the gap between Year 2 and Year 3, this range is perfect for introducing and consolidating comprehension skills throughout Key Stage One. The books introduce a wide variety of topics, and their rich and varied subject matter will appeal to most pupils.

Year 1

This book introduces and reinforces fundamental comprehension skills. It begins with accessible image-based activities and progresses to questions based around short fiction and non-fiction texts. These engaging and accessible texts are drawn from a variety of genres including rhymes, fairy tales and letters.

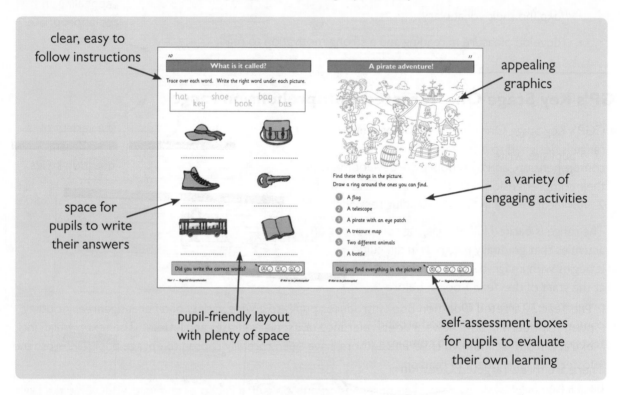

clear, easy to follow instructions

appealing graphics

space for pupils to write their answers

a variety of engaging activities

pupil-friendly layout with plenty of space

self-assessment boxes for pupils to evaluate their own learning

- The activities throughout the Year 1 Targeted Question Book have been carefully designed to capture pupils' interest as they enter Key Stage One. The pages are clearly laid out to ensure that they are appealing and accessible for early readers.

- The book tests a range of comprehension skills, such as matching, grouping, sequencing, predicting, reasoning, fact retrieval and inference.

Using the Year 1 Targeted Question Book

- The Year 1 Targeted Question Book gradually progresses in difficulty, so ensure that pupils work though the activities in order. When using the book in Guided Reading sessions, encourage pupils to read the instructions for each activity carefully, using phonic knowledge to sound out words where necessary. Make sure pupils have understood the instructions before they attempt to complete the activities.

- Self-assessment boxes have been included on each page so that pupils can evaluate their own learning. Pupils should be encouraged to fill these in once they have completed each page. The boxes can be used alongside the pupil progress charts to track pupils' development throughout the year.

- Once pupils have completed the activities in their books, you can move on to the Extra Activity suggestions in the Teacher Book (see pages 5-6). Many of these build upon pupils' responses in the Question Book.

The Targeted Question Books

Year 2

This book consolidates the comprehension skills that pupils have learnt in Year 1. The book progresses from short, simple extracts to longer and more complex texts. More advanced comprehension skills are gradually introduced and strengthened through the inclusion of increasingly challenging and open-ended questions.

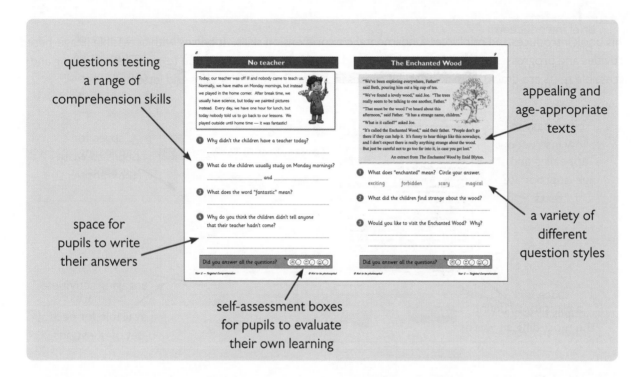

questions testing a range of comprehension skills

appealing and age-appropriate texts

space for pupils to write their answers

a variety of different question styles

self-assessment boxes for pupils to evaluate their own learning

- The Year 2 Targeted Question Book introduces pupils to a wide variety of different genres, including poetry, modern fiction, news articles, reference texts, diary entries and letters. The texts, which include extracts from well-known children's authors, have been carefully chosen to engage pupils' interest and foster their enjoyment of reading.

- Each text is followed by a set of comprehension questions that reinforce and further develop the skills learnt in Year 1. Some questions require pupils to draw on their own opinions and experiences, encouraging them to relate to the texts on a personal level.

Using the Year 2 Targeted Question Book

- Make sure pupils work through the Year 2 Targeted Question Book in order. During Guided Reading sessions, encourage pupils to read the text thoroughly before tackling the questions. It may be useful to explore the meaning of new vocabulary with students to ensure they fully understand the text. Once pupils are familiar with the content, ask them to read the questions and revisit the text to pick out the key details they need to answer the questions.

- Encourage pupils to fill in the self assessment boxes at the bottom of each page. These can be used as an indicator of pupils' engagement with the questions and, along with the pupil progress charts, can help you to track pupils' progress during the year.

- You can move on to the extra activities in the Teacher Book once pupils have completed the questions. Some of these activities are suitable for pupils to complete individually if they finish the questions earlier than their classmates. Many of the activities build upon pupils' answers to questions in the Question Book or open up discussions about important aspects of the text.

The Targeted Question Books

Year 3 Ready

This book bridges the gap between Year 2 and Year 3. It introduces longer, more challenging texts from many different genres. The varied and engaging questions build upon the comprehension skills introduced in the Year 2 book and equip pupils to tackle the challenges of reading comprehension at Key Stage Two.

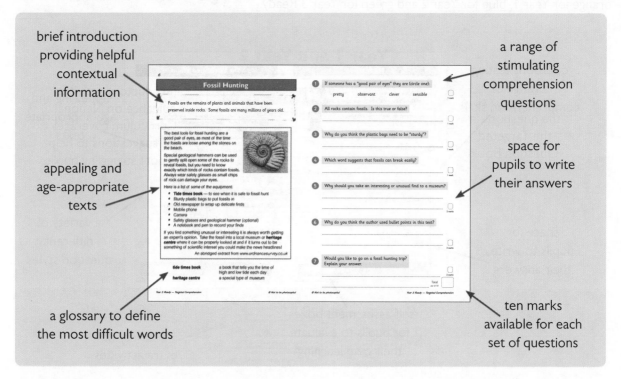

brief introduction providing helpful contextual information

appealing and age-appropriate texts

a glossary to define the most difficult words

a range of stimulating comprehension questions

space for pupils to write their answers

ten marks available for each set of questions

- The Year 3 Ready Targeted Question Book includes a range of fiction, non-fiction and poetry texts, and introduces pupils to some new genres such as plays, classic fiction and folk tales. They are taken from age-appropriate sources that will inspire many pupils to read the rest of the text independently.

- Each text is followed by a set of challenging and stimulating comprehension questions which will test and strengthen skills developed throughout Years 1 and 2.

Using the Year 3 Ready Targeted Question Book

- At the start of your Guided Reading sessions, make sure pupils read the introduction to the text carefully. These introductions provide useful information about the text and its author, or about the context in which it was written. This background information is important for pupils' understanding of the text.

- A glossary is provided with some texts, defining the most challenging words. You may want to encourage pupils to look up any other unfamiliar words in a dictionary and check answers to vocabulary-based questions themselves.

- The comprehension questions are marked out of ten. You can record pupils' marks in the pupil progress charts (see page 5) to help you track the development of their comprehension skills.

- Once pupils have completed the questions, move on to the Extra Activity suggestions provided for each page.

- The Year 3 Ready Targeted Question Book ends with a 'your turn' activity, which challenges pupils to write their own text and construct a series of questions about it. This will further develop pupils' literacy skills and give them a new perspective on text comprehension. It will also allow you to see how well pupils' comprehension skills have progressed.

The Teacher Book — Years 1 and 2

This Teacher Book will help you to use the Targeted Question Books to their full potential, incorporating the texts and activities from all three books into your lesson plans. It provides full answers to every activity and question from the Targeted Question Books, as well as suggestions for varied extra activities. To help you find the information you need quickly and easily, the Teacher Book pages are colour-coded to match the colour of the Question Books — orange for Year 1, blue for Year 2 and green for Year 3 Ready.

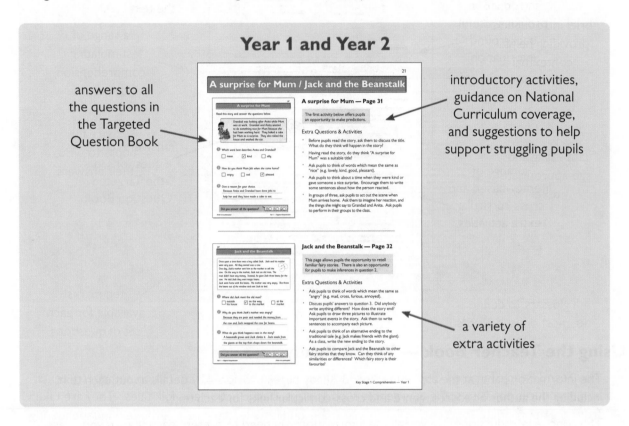

answers to all the questions in the Targeted Question Book

introductory activities, guidance on National Curriculum coverage, and suggestions to help support struggling pupils

a variety of extra activities

Using the Teacher Book — Years 1 and 2

- The extra activities for Year 1 and Year 2 tend to have a literacy focus and are linked to the text or activity.

- Some activities can be used as extension work for pupils who complete the comprehension questions quickly. Others can be done by the class as a whole, developing skills such as working in groups, presenting ideas and listening to classmates.

- Many of the extra activities open up the opportunity for further exploration of the topics addressed in the Targeted Question Book.

Monitoring Pupils' Progress

- Pupil progress charts containing the title of each activity and a space for pupils' names are provided on pages 49-52. These will allow you to record and track pupils' progress and their level of engagement with each activity throughout the year.

- A key is provided to help you record each pupil's performance using a scale from 1-3. You should give pupils a score based on how much assistance they required to complete the activities. 1 signifies that pupils required a lot of assistance, while 3 signifies that they were able to complete the activities independently.

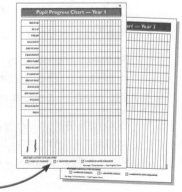

The Teacher Book — Year 3 Ready

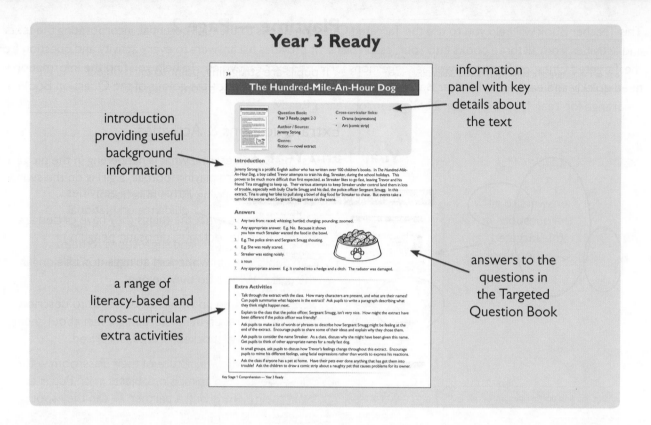

Year 3 Ready

introduction providing useful background information

information panel with key details about the text

a range of literacy-based and cross-curricular extra activities

answers to the questions in the Targeted Question Book

Using the Teacher Book — Year 3 Ready

- The information panel at the top of the Year 3 Ready pages provides key details about each text, including the author or source, genre and cross-curricular links for each text.

- The concise introductions give you all the information you need to present each text to your class, highlighting important facts and concepts that pupils should be aware of before they start reading. Some also provide a useful starter activity to help you introduce the topic to the class.

- Extra activities are included on each page, with ideas for literacy-based activities as well as activities that link to other areas of the Key Stage One curriculum.

Marking Pupils' Work

- There are ten marks available for each set of questions in the Question Book. You can record each pupil's marks for each text in the pupil progress chart on page 53. This will enable you to easily monitor their performance as they work through the Question Book.

- The Teacher Book provides answers to all the questions in the Question Book.

- Answers preceded by "E.g." require pupils to offer their own interpretation of the information contained in the text. There is often no 'correct answer', but pupils' answers should be based on the text and go into a similar amount of detail to the sample answer.

- Answers marked "Any appropriate answer" require pupils to offer their own opinions. Again, there is no 'correct answer', and the answers given in the Teacher Book are just suggestions. However, pupils should show a clear understanding of the question and give reasons to support their answer.

Playtime / Where do they live?

Playtime — Page 2

If pupils are struggling, point to each object and ask, "Does this belong in a park?"

Extra Questions & Activities

- Ask pupils to describe what is happening in the picture (e.g. the boys are playing football, a girl is on the swing, another girl is playing with a hula hoop).

- Do pupils know what the things they have circled are called? (Giraffe, octopus, dinosaur, penguin.)

- Can pupils explain why these animals don't belong in the park? Where do they belong?

- As a group, come up with a list of words to describe how the children in the picture might feel about seeing the animals, e.g. shocked, scared, surprised.

- Ask pupils to draw a picture of their classroom with some unexpected animals or objects in it. Pupils can swap their picture with a partner — can they spot the things that don't belong?

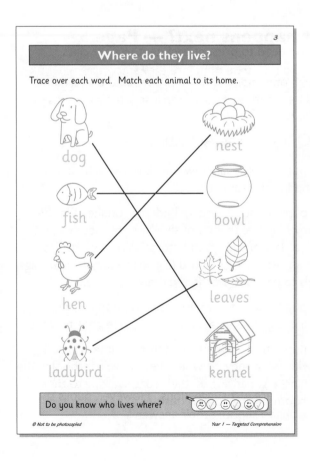

Where do they live? — Page 3

This exercise allows pupils to draw upon their own knowledge of animals and their homes.

Extra Questions & Activities

- Ask pupils if they can think of any other homes for the animals on the page (e.g. fish also live in the sea, hens also live in barns, some dogs might live indoors).

- Show pupils pictures of animal homes, e.g. a hive, a stable. Can they guess which animals live there?

- Go through the alphabet and ask pupils to point to each letter from the words beneath the pictures, e.g. the 'a' in ladybird, the 'b' in bowl. Which letters don't appear in the words on the page (c, j, m, p, q, u, x and z)? Can pupils think of words that contain these missing letters?

- The word 'ladybird' is a compound word. Explain that compound words are two words that have been put together to make a new word. Can pupils think of any other compound words (e.g. playground, football)?

At the beach / What happens next?

At the beach — Page 4

Children should have coloured the items that have been circled.

Extra Questions & Activities

- Ask pupils if there is anything else they might take to the beach. Ask them to write a list or draw pictures.

- Ask pupils to imagine that they are swimming in the sea with a snorkelling mask. What can they see underwater? Ask them to draw a picture. You could hand out sheets with printed snorkelling frames so that their pictures look as though they are being seen through the mask.

- Teach pupils the tongue twister 'She Sells Sea Shells'. Practise as a class and see who can say it all the way through with no mistakes.

- Show pupils how to loosely draw around their hands to make a shell shape. Ask them to write a sentence on their shell about their favourite thing to do at the beach. The shells could form a class display.

What happens next? — Page 5

Although one ending is more probable, the alternative should be accepted if pupils can justify their response.

Extra Questions & Activities

- Ask pupils to explain how they knew which picture finished each sequence.

- Ask pupils about their own bedtime routine. Do they do anything else that is not shown in the pictures (e.g. drink a glass of milk, read a story)? Write words from their answers on the board (e.g. milk, story). Encourage pupils to copy the words and draw a picture.

- Ask pupils to write or verbalise a caption for each picture, e.g. 'He brushes his teeth.', 'He goes to sleep.'

- Ask pupils to draw their own three-frame cartoon showing what they do when they arrive at school in the morning, e.g. hanging up their coat, walking to their classroom, sitting at their desk.

Finish the group / What is for dinner?

Finish the group — Page 6

Pupils may have drawn different pictures to those suggested. Any sensible alternatives should be rewarded.

Extra Questions & Activities

- Ask pupils to draw or write down any other things which would fit into each category from the exercise.

- Give pupils other categories, e.g. vegetables, sports, things that live underwater. How many things can they think of that fit each category?

- Ask pupils about the fruit on the page. Do they know what they are called? What fruit do pupils like to eat?

- Ask pupils if they know the names of the animals on the page. Do they know what countries they are from?

- Using the list of birthday party objects from the first activity, ask children to describe an imaginary birthday party. What can pupils see, hear, smell, touch and taste?

What is for dinner? — Page 7

If pupils are struggling, ask them to describe what is happening in each picture before putting them in order.

Extra Questions & Activities

- Talk to pupils about the order they have put the pictures in. How did they decide on the order?

- Ask pupils to write or verbalise a sentence which describes each frame of the story.

- Ask pupils what might have happened before the first picture (e.g. they might have gone to the shops to buy ingredients, they might have washed their hands) and after the last picture (e.g. they might have washed the dishes). Pupils could draw a picture to accompany one of these new steps.

- Ask pupils to draw their own storyboard about what they do during lunchtime at school. Ask them to cut it out and give it to a partner to re-order.

In my pencil case / What is the order?

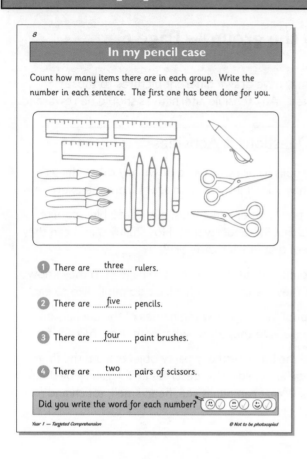

In my pencil case — Page 8

Encourage pupils who are struggling to number each item as they count them. Struggling pupils may also complete the sentences using digits.

Extra Questions & Activities

- Ask pupils to circle all the plural words on the page.

- Instruct pupils to colour the pencils in green, the scissors in purple, the rulers in red, the brushes in blue and the pen in yellow.

- Ask pupils to make a list of all the other things that might be found in a pencil case, e.g. a rubber, felt tips, a sharpener, paperclips.

- As a group, make a list of words that rhyme with 'pen', e.g. men, hen, den, ten.

- Ask pupils to design a pencil case. Encourage them to be creative with their designs, for example they could have secret pockets or incorporate different sections for each type of stationery.

What is the order? — Page 9

Ask pupils to identify each image before beginning the activity.

Extra Questions & Activities

- Ask pupils to explain how they knew what order each step came in. What would happen if they did the actions in the wrong order?

- Can pupils explain why it is important to give instructions in the right order? Would it be easy or hard to follow a recipe that was mixed up?

- Ask pupils to write a list of words to describe each picture, e.g. the pizza might be hot, tasty, yummy.

- Ask pupils to choose a picture from the page and describe each step, e.g. Put the bread in the toaster. Spread butter on the toast. Eat the toast.

- Ask pupils to mime one of the activities — the rest of the class can guess what they are acting out.

What is it called? / A pirate adventure!

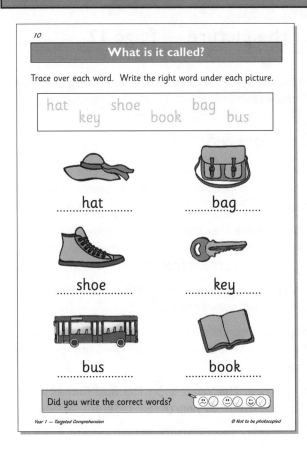

What is it called? — Page 10

Ask pupils to read the words out loud before starting the activity.

Extra Questions & Activities

* Ask pupils to circle the words that begin with 'b'. Can they think of any other words that begin with 'b'? Ask them to write a list, then compare their list with a partner. Have they spelt everything right? Did their partner think of any words they didn't know?

* Ask pupils to colour in all the items from the page that can be worn. Can they think of any other examples of things you can wear?

* Ask pupils to change the spellings of each object on the page to make all the words plural.

* Ask pupils to come up with words to describe each object, e.g. the girl's hat, a red bag, a dirty shoe.

* Can pupils come up with a story that includes all the objects from the page?

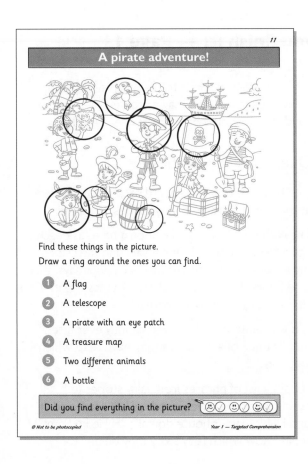

A pirate adventure! — Page 11

Pupils may need help reading the words 'telescope' and 'eye patch'.

Extra Questions & Activities

* Ask pupils to describe what is happening in the picture.

* Can pupils label some of the other objects in the picture (e.g. a barrel, a ship, a palm tree, a spade)?

* Would pupils like to meet the pirates in the picture? Why or why not?

* Ask pupils to create a wanted poster for an imaginary pirate. Pupils can draw their pirate and add a description of their crimes underneath their drawing. It may be useful to print off a wanted poster template to hand out.

* Tell pupils about messages in bottles. In small groups, ask pupils to write a message, put it in a plastic bottle and then hide it in the classroom. Pupils can hunt for other groups' bottles.

Colour the picture / Can you finish it?

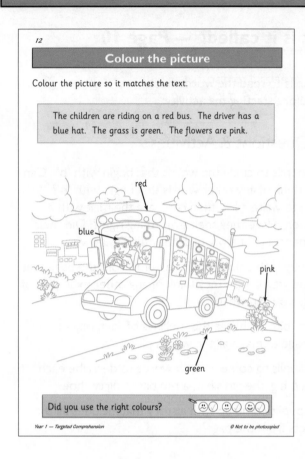

Colour the picture — Page 12

This exercise provides an opportunity to complement the curriculum by teaching 'The Wheels On The Bus' song.

Extra Questions & Activities

- Ask pupils to colour in the rest of the picture and to write some sentences to continue the description on the page, e.g. The sky is blue. The clouds are white.

- Ask pupils where they think the bus is going. Are the children on their way to school? Are they going on a class trip? Can pupils justify their responses?

- Have pupils ever been on a bus? Where did they go? Did they enjoy travelling by bus?

- Ask pupils to imagine that they are travelling on a bus. Ask them to describe what they can see from the window.

- Teach the song 'The Wheels On The Bus' to the class. Can they learn it off by heart?

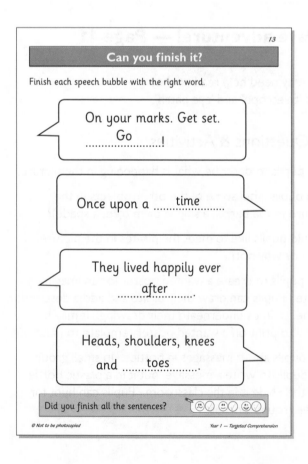

Can you finish it? — Page 13

This activity enables children to recognise and complete predictable phrases. Pupils may need help spelling 'toes', as it sounds like it should be the split o-e digraph.

Extra Questions & Activities

- Ask pupils where they have heard each phrase before, e.g. at the start of a race, in fairy stories, in a song.

- Starting with the phrase 'Once upon a time', ask each pupil to add one sentence, and go around the class making a story. Write down what each pupil says, then read the finished story to the class. Do they like it? Can they think of any ways to improve it?

- Discuss the sentence 'They lived happily ever after.' Can pupils think of any stories they have read which end this way?

- Give pupils a list of phrases from fairy stories (e.g. "What big teeth you have Grandma!"; "I'll huff and I'll puff and I'll blow your house down!"; "Fi Fie Fo Fum!"). Do pupils know which fairy story they belong to?

Key Stage 1 Comprehension — Year 1

In the park / Yes or no?

In the park — Page 14

It may be helpful to discuss what is happening in the picture before pupils attempt the activity.

Extra Questions & Activities

- Ask pupils to look at the expressions on the children's faces. Ask pupils to think of a word to describe how each child might be feeling.

- What else can pupils see in the park (e.g. a lake, a treehouse, a tyre swing)? How is this park different or similar to their local park?

- Ask pupils to pick one of the characters from the picture and think up a story about them and what they are doing in the park.

- Ask pupils what other things they can do in the park (e.g. play football, have a picnic, play in the playground) and write a list on the board. Have a class vote to see which activity is the most popular.

Yes or no? — Page 15

Before starting the activity, ask pupils to describe the people they can see on the page.

Extra Questions & Activities

- Ask children to draw pictures that match the sentences where 'no' has been circled, i.e. "Laura dressed up as a princess" and "Luke is a doctor". They could also correct the sentences that don't match the original pictures, i.e. "Laura dressed up as a pirate" and "Luke is a farmer."

- Ask pupils to come up with a story explaining how Barry hurt himself.

- Ask the children to play 'Guess Who' using the characters on the page. Ask one pupil to the front of the class and assign them one of the characters. Get the rest of the class to ask 'yes' or 'no' questions in order to ascertain who the pupil at the front is pretending to be, e.g. Have you got a broken leg? Are you wearing glasses? You could then expand this game of 'Guess Who' so that pupils have to guess the identity of a classmate using 'yes' and 'no' questions.

Read the sign / Finish the sentences

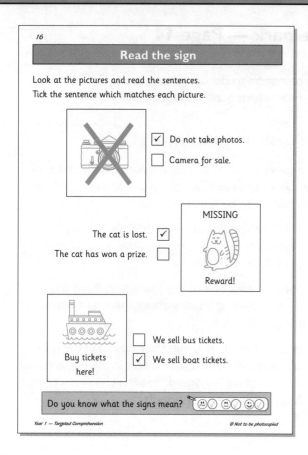

Read the sign — Page 16

Pupils may need assistance with the first sign. Talk to pupils about what they can see in the image and what the cross might signify.

Extra Questions & Activities

- Ask pupils to draw signs to represent the other options in the activity, (i.e "Camera for sale", "The cat has won a prize", "We sell bus tickets").

- Show pupils some examples of signs from around the school (e.g. wash your hands, school crossing). Do they know what these signs mean?

- Discuss the conventions of signs with pupils, e.g. big pictures, usually in bold colours, not many words. Why do pupils think signs look this way? (E.g. They're designed to catch people's attention, not using words means that anyone can understand them.)

- Ask children to design their own poster or sign. It might advertise the next school play, or it might remind pupils not to run in the corridors.

Finish the sentences — Page 17

Pupils should read the exercise carefully to avoid confusion over the different children.

Extra Questions & Activities

- Ask pupils to label the animals in the picture.

- Ask pupils to write sentences about Lucy and her pets. For example, they could write: Lucy is playing with two squirrels; There are two squirrels climbing on Lucy. (You may need to help children spell 'squirrels'.)

- Pupils could colour in the picture on the page.

- Ask pupils to look at the dog in the picture. What do they think the dog might do next (e.g. jump in the lake, chase the frog)? Ask pupils to give reasons for their answers.

- Ask pupils to write a sentence about their own pets, or the clothes they are wearing.

- Ask pupils what they think the weather is like in the picture. Ask them to give reasons for their answers (e.g. it is warm because Patrick is wearing shorts).

Who am I? / Who said what?

Who am I? — Page 18

Support students who are struggling by asking them to read the sentences and describe each object in their own words.

Extra Questions & Activities

- Ask pupils to write or verbalise similar sentences for the other objects on the page (e.g. 'you use me to score a goal'). They could swap sentences with a partner and guess which object is being described. Then give each pupil a picture of an object that isn't on the page. In turn, ask them to say a sentence describing it. Ask the class to guess what they are. Pupils can ask extra questions if they are struggling to guess the object.

- Ask pupils to look at the camping pictures and imagine that they are on a camping holiday. What is the weather like? What animals might they be able to see? Ask them to write or verbalise some sentences about waking up outside in a tent. What is it like?

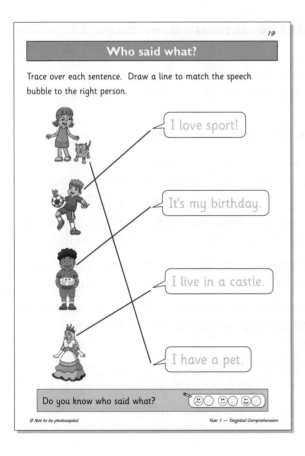

Who said what? — Page 19

This page offers an opportunity for pupils to develop their inference skills. If pupils are struggling, ask them what they can see in each picture.

Extra Questions & Activities

- Ask pupils to explain why they matched each character with each speech bubble.

- Ask pupils to draw a self-portrait and write some speech bubbles which describe themselves. They could write about their appearance, their interests or any facts about themselves. You could turn the pictures and speech bubbles into a class display.

- Ask pupils to pick one of the characters from the exercise and write or verbalise a short description or story related to that character.

- In pairs, ask pupils to take turns trying to mime actions for each of the characters (e.g. they could pretend to stroke an imaginary pet for 'I have a pet', or blow out the candles on a birthday cake for 'It's my birthday').

Little Miss Muffet / Match the sentence

Little Miss Muffet — Page 20

This page and the accompanying activities provide an opportunity for pupils to become familiar with a rhyme and to learn it off by heart.

Extra Questions & Activities

- Do pupils know what "tuffet", "curds" and "whey" mean? If not, can they make a sensible guess? Look up the words in a dictionary to check.

- Can pupils identify the words that rhyme in the song? Ask them to circle them. Can they think of a different ending that also rhymes (e.g. "and asked if she wanted to play")?

- Talk to pupils about why Miss Muffet ran away. Are they scared of spiders too? Why or why not?

- In small groups, ask pupils to act out what happens in the nursery rhyme.

- Ask pupils to learn the rhyme off by heart. Repeat it in class until pupils can recite it themselves.

Match the sentence — Page 21

Encourage pupils who are struggling to look carefully at the pictures and the speech bubbles.

Extra Questions & Activities

- Ask pupils to justify their answers. What clues did they use from the pictures to make their decision (e.g. Lewis is smiling, so he's enjoying making the model)?

- Can pupils circle the two exclamation marks used on the page? Do they know why they have been used?

- Ask pupils to circle all the words from the page which end with 's'. Which of these words are plurals?

- Ask pupils to draw pictures to represent the incorrect sentences (e.g. "Jessica has lost her dog").

Spot the odd one out / Read the menu

Spot the odd one out — Page 22

This activity allows pupils to check that what they read makes sense in the context of each picture.

Extra Questions & Activities

- Ask pupils to explain why they circled each sentence.

- Ask pupils to think up a story about Liam and Arthur. Why do they have a map and a camera? Are they going on holiday or on an adventure? What happens?

- Ask pupils to write their own set of three sentences to accompany each picture, so that one of them is an odd one out. For example, they could write: Arthur had a backpack. Liam took a photo. Emma ate a sandwich.

- Ask pupils to draw a picture to match each odd sentence.

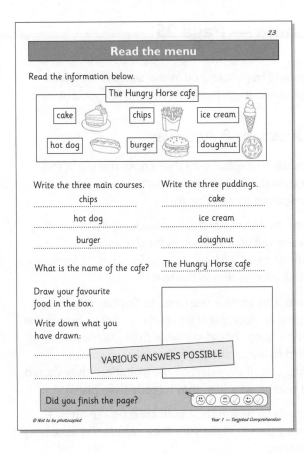

Read the menu — Page 23

Read the items on the menu aloud with the class before starting the activity. Students may need assistance with words like 'doughnut' and 'courses'.

Extra Questions & Activities

- Ask pupils to write down what they would order from the cafe and give a reason for their choice.

- Ask pupils how they recognised this as a menu (e.g. it isn't written in full sentences, there are pictures next to each item). What else might they expect to find on a menu (e.g. the price, a description of each item)?

- Ask pupils to write two words to describe each item from the menu, e.g. cake might be sweet and tasty. Compile the words into a word bank.

- Ask pupils to imagine they are a chef creating a brand new dish. Ask them to draw it and label it. Do they think everyone will like it? Why or why not?

Reasons / Party time

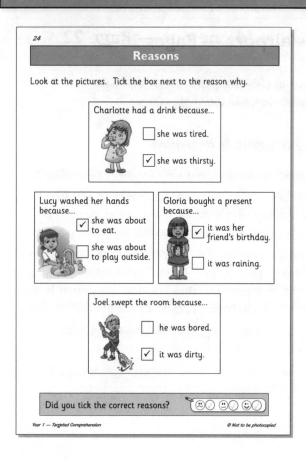

Reasons — Page 24

Although some answers are more probable than others, alternative responses should be accepted if pupils can justify their reasoning.

Extra Questions & Activities

- Ask pupils to explain why they ticked each box.

- Ask pupils to write a sentence to explain the reasons that haven't been ticked, e.g. Charlotte went to bed because she was tired.

- Ask pupils to circle all the capital letters on the page. Why do those words have capital letters?

- Ask pupils to imagine what present Gloria bought for her friend. Ask pupils to write about the best present they have ever received.

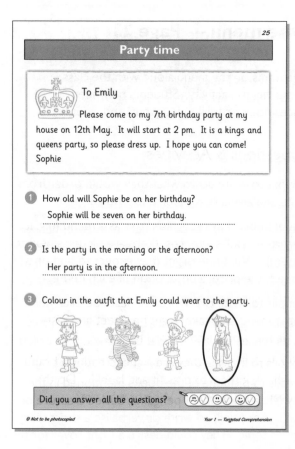

Party time — Page 25

Pupils should have coloured in the outfit circled on the page. Encourage pupils to write in full sentences.

Extra Questions & Activities

- Ask pupils to explain why they chose the outfit for Emily to wear. What kind of party would the other three options be suitable for?

- Discuss the format of the text with pupils. Have they ever received an invitation before? Explain that invitations need a date, time and location. Can pupils spot this information in the text?

- Ask pupils to write a response to Sophie, either accepting or declining the invitation. If they accept the invitation, they should say what they are most looking forward to about the party (e.g. playing games, dressing up). If they decline the invitation, they should give a reason why (e.g. they already have plans).

- Ask pupils to design their own invitation to an imaginary party. Make sure they include the necessary information.

At the airport / My favourite books

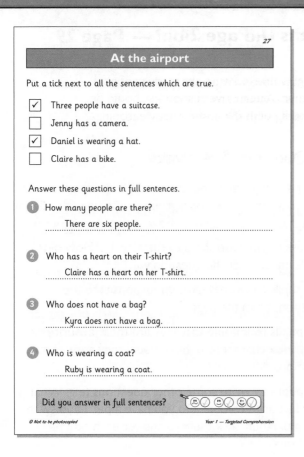

At the airport — Pages 26-27

Allow pupils who are struggling to complete the activity with one word answers.

Extra Questions & Activities

- Ask pupils to write a couple of sentences describing Jack and Jenny. Pupils might describe what they are wearing or what they are holding.

- Ask pupils to look at the clothes the people in the activity are wearing. Who do they think is travelling to somewhere hot? Who do they think is travelling to somewhere cold? Ask them to justify their answers (e.g. Ruby is wearing gloves so she is going somewhere cold).

- Ask pupils if they have ever been on an aeroplane. What was it like? Did they enjoy it or not?

- Ask pupils to choose one of the characters from the page and to imagine a story about their holiday.

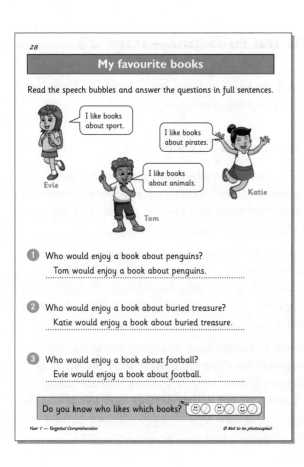

My favourite books — Page 28

This page assesses pupils' ability to make inferences. Pupils may need help reading the words 'penguins' and 'buried treasure'.

Extra Questions & Activities

- Ask pupils to explain their answers to each question. How did they know who would like each book?

- Explain the difference between fiction and non-fiction. Can pupils think of book recommendations for Evie, Tom and Katie? Pupils could go to the school library to look for suitable books. E.g. Tom might like *Spot the Dog* or *The Very Hungry Caterpillar*.

- Ask pupils about their favourite book. Get them to write some sentences explaining what their favourite book is and why they like it.

- Ask pupils to pick one of the books mentioned in the activity (i.e. a book about penguins, buried treasure or football). Ask pupils to write or verbalise a short story about this topic. They could design a front cover for their chosen book.

What is the question? / A postcard to Gran

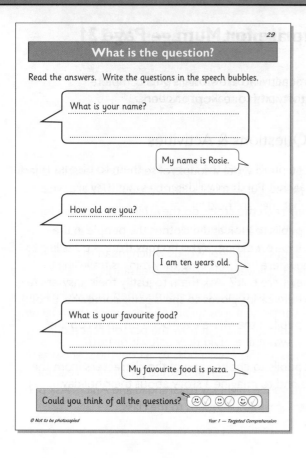

What is the question? — Page 29

Pupils may have written alternative questions. Accept any that could make sense with the answer provided.

Extra Questions & Activities

- This page gives an opportunity to discuss questions and question marks. As a group, come up with a list of question words (e.g. what, how, why, when, where).

- Discuss pupils' responses to the activity. How did pupils know what the question was?

- Ask pupils to write their own responses to the questions from the page.

- Ask pupils to imagine that they are their favourite storybook character — how would they answer the questions differently?

- Ask pupils to write some other questions (e.g. What is your favourite colour? Do you have a pet?) and swap with a partner. Ask them to answer each other's questions.

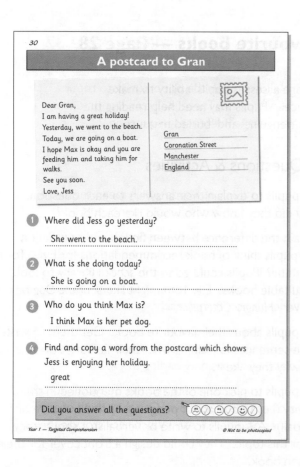

A postcard to Gran — Page 30

Question 3 gives pupils an opportunity to make inferences.

Extra Questions & Activities

- Discuss pupils' answers to question 3. Why did they choose that answer? What evidence from the text did they use? Ask them to underline the parts of the text that helped them decide who Max was.

- Discuss the format of the text with pupils. How do they know that it is a postcard? What features can they identify (e.g. space for an address, a stamp, starting with 'Dear' and ending with 'Love'). Ask them to label these features on the postcard.

- Ask pupils to create their own postcard using the features they have just identified. They should write to a friend or relative about a real or imagined holiday. Where did they go? What did they do? What was the weather like? Pupils should draw a picture of their holiday destination on the front of the postcard.

A surprise for Mum / Jack and the Beanstalk

31

A surprise for Mum

Read this story and answer the questions below.

Grandad was looking after Anita while Mum was at work. Grandad and Anita wanted to do something nice for Mum because she had been working hard. They baked a cake for Mum as a surprise. They also tidied the house and washed the car.

1 Which word best describes Anita and Grandad?

☐ mean ☑ kind ☐ silly

2 How do you think Mum felt when she came home?

☐ angry ☐ sad ☑ pleased

3 Give a reason for your choice.

Because Anita and Grandad have done jobs to
help her and they have made a cake to eat.

Did you answer all the questions? ☺☺☺☺☺

© Not to be photocopied   *Year 1 — Targeted Comprehension*

A surprise for Mum — Page 31

The first activity below offers pupils an opportunity to make predictions.

Extra Questions & Activities

- Before pupils read the story, ask them to discuss the title. What do they think will happen in the story?

- Having read the story, do they think "A surprise for Mum" was a suitable title?

- Ask pupils to think of words which mean the same as "nice" (e.g. lovely, kind, good, pleasant).

- Ask pupils to think about a time when they were kind or gave someone a nice surprise. Encourage them to write some sentences about how the person reacted.

- In groups of three, ask pupils to act out the scene when Mum arrives home. Ask them to imagine her reaction, and the things she might say to Grandad and Anita. Ask pupils to perform in their groups to the class.

32

Jack and the Beanstalk

Once upon a time there was a boy called Jack. Jack and his mother were very poor. All they owned was a cow.
One day, Jack's mother sent him to the market to sell the cow. On the way to the market, Jack met an old man. The man didn't have any money. Instead, he gave Jack three beans for the cow. He told Jack they were magic beans.
Jack went home with the beans. His mother was very angry. She threw the beans out of the window and sent Jack to bed.

1 Where did Jack meet the old man?

☐ outside his house ☑ on the way to the market ☐ at the market

2 Why do you think Jack's mother was angry?

Because they are poor and needed the money from
the cow and Jack swapped the cow for beans.

3 What do you think happens next in the story?

A beanstalk grows and Jack climbs it. Jack steals from
the giants at the top then chops down the beanstalk.

Did you answer all the questions? ☺☺☺☺☺

Year 1 — Targeted Comprehension   © Not to be photocopied

Jack and the Beanstalk — Page 32

This page allows pupils the opportunity to retell familiar fairy stories. There is also an opportunity for pupils to make inferences in question 2.

Extra Questions & Activities

- Ask pupils to think of words which mean the same as "angry" (e.g. mad, cross, furious, annoyed).

- Discuss pupils' answers to question 3. Did anybody write anything different? How does the story end? Ask pupils to draw three pictures to illustrate important events in the story. Ask them to write sentences to accompany each picture.

- Ask pupils to think of an alternative ending to the traditional tale (e.g. Jack makes friends with the giant). As a class, write the new ending to the story.

- Ask pupils to compare Jack and the Beanstalk to other fairy stories that they know. Can they think of any similarities or differences? Which fairy story is their favourite?

How to use the answers / How to grow a seed

How to use the answers

- This section provides answers to all the questions in the Year 2 Pupil Book.

- The answers provided throughout this section are intended as a guide only. You will need to use your own judgement to decide whether the answers pupils have given are correct.

- Answers preceded by "E.g." require pupils to give their own interpretation of the information contained in the text or to offer their own opinions. Alternative answers should be accepted as long as pupils can justify their answers and explain their reasoning.

- Encourage pupils to answer all the questions using full sentences, and to think carefully about spelling, punctuation and grammar. Pupils who are struggling should be allowed to complete the activities using one word answers. You can also use the suggestions in the blue boxes at the start of each section to give pupils extra support.

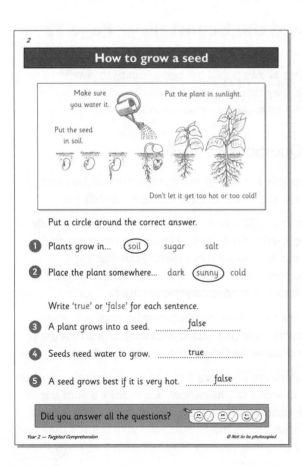

How to grow a seed — Page 2

If pupils are struggling, encourage them to describe what is happening in the pictures before answering the questions.

Extra Questions & Activities

- Ask the class why people plant seeds. Make a list on the board of pupils' answers (e.g. to grow flowers for gardens, to grow vegetables to eat).

- As a class, plant some seeds to test whether the information in the text is correct. Put the seeds in a variety of places, such as on a windowsill, in a dark cupboard and in a fridge. What differences do the class notice in how the seeds grow in each place?

- Ask the class to think of some uses for plants. Give each child a picture of an everyday object (e.g. a piece of paper, a cotton t-shirt, a metal drinks can). Ask them to identify whether or not their item comes from a plant. Discuss their answers as a class — are they correct? Which plants do their objects come from?

Making lemonade / The Owl and the Pussy-cat

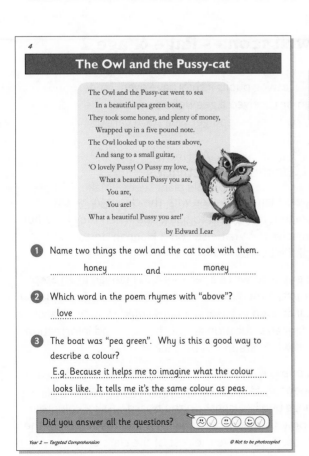

Making lemonade

3

Lemonade Recipe

You will need: 3 lemons, 100g sugar and 1 litre of water.

How to make:
- Squeeze the lemons so the juice goes into a large jug.
- Add the sugar to the lemon juice.
- Pour the water into the jug and stir until everything is mixed together.
- Add some ice cubes and enjoy your lemonade!

1 What is a "recipe"?

E.g. A list of instructions for making food or drink.

2 How many lemons do you need for this recipe?

You need three lemons.

3 Write the number 1, 2, 3, 4 or 5 next to each sentence to show the right order. The first one has been done for you.

| 2 | Add the sugar. | 5 | Add some ice. | 3 | Add the water. |
| 4 | Mix it together. | 1 | Squeeze the lemons into a jug. |

Did you answer all the questions? 😦◯ 😐✓ 😊◯

© Not to be photocopied   Year 2 — Targeted Comprehension

Making lemonade — Page 3

Encourage pupils who are struggling with question 3 to number the steps in the recipe and then match the steps to the sentences in the question.

Extra Questions & Activities

- As a class, think of words that might describe the taste of the lemonade and write them on the board (e.g. sweet, bitter, delicious). Ask pupils to create a poster advertising the lemonade. They should include a sentence describing how it tastes.

- Ask pupils about what they like to eat or drink on hot days. Ask them to write some sentences explaining why their chosen items help them to cool down.

- Tell pupils that you want to make five jugs of the lemonade. As a class, work out how much of each ingredient you will need.

- Use the recipe to make lemonade. Pupils could market their lemonade using the posters from the first activity.

The Owl and the Pussy-cat

4

The Owl and the Pussy-cat went to sea
In a beautiful pea green boat,
They took some honey, and plenty of money,
Wrapped up in a five pound note.
The Owl looked up to the stars above,
And sang to a small guitar,
'O lovely Pussy! O Pussy my love,
What a beautiful Pussy you are,
You are,
You are!
What a beautiful Pussy you are!'

by Edward Lear

1 Name two things the owl and the cat took with them.

honey and money

2 Which word in the poem rhymes with "above"?

love

3 The boat was "pea green". Why is this a good way to describe a colour?

E.g. Because it helps me to imagine what the colour looks like. It tells me it's the same colour as peas.

Did you answer all the questions? 😦◯ 😐◯ 😊◯

Year 2 — Targeted Comprehension   © Not to be photocopied

The Owl and the Pussy-cat — Page 4

Pupils may also have given "five pound note" or "guitar" as answers to question 1.

Extra Questions & Activities

- Ask pupils if they enjoyed the poem. Get them to write some sentences explaining what they liked or didn't like about it.

- Ask pupils to think about what might happen next. Ask them to discuss their ideas with a partner and then write some sentences describing what they think is going to happen. Finish by reading the rest of the poem to the class.

- Discuss pupils' answers to question 3. Can they think of any other ways to describe colours? Make a list of examples on the board (e.g. sky blue, rose red, sunflower yellow).

- The Owl and the Pussy-cat take money, a guitar and honey with them on their trip. Ask pupils to write a list of five things they would take with them if they were going on a long journey. Discuss with them why they chose each item.

Seasons / Get well soon

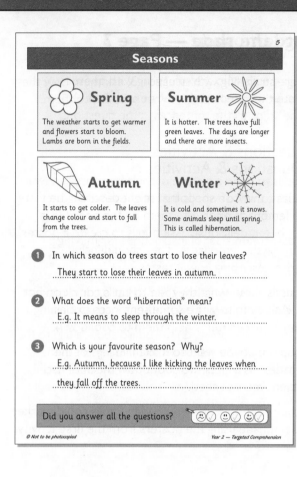

Seasons — Page 5

Begin the activity by asking pupils if they know the names of the four seasons. Can they put them in order?

Extra Questions & Activities

- Ask pupils about which season it currently is. How do they know? Which season will come next? Ask pupils to write another sentence about each season.

- Ask pupils to write a list of three items of clothing that they might wear in each season. Discuss their answers.

- Ask pupils to share their answers to question 3. As a class, discuss what pupils enjoy or don't enjoy about each season. Ask pupils to create a collage of their favourite season. They could collect materials outside to use in their collage, or bring items and pictures from home.

- Hand out brightly coloured paper to pupils. Ask them to draw around their hands and cut them out. Encourage pupils to write sentences about spring on their handprints. Arrange the handprints in circles to make flowers, and add a stem and some leaves to each one. Display the flowers around the classroom.

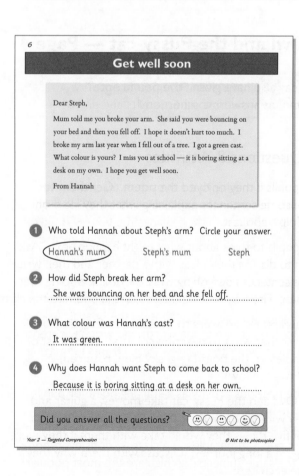

Get well soon — Page 6

Begin by asking pupils if they have ever written or received a get well soon card. When do people send get well soon cards?

Extra Questions & Activities

- Discuss Hannah's letter with the class. Why is it important to be kind to someone when they have hurt themselves? What else could Hannah do to make Steph feel better?

- Ask pupils to write a response to Hannah from Steph. Encourage them to think about the language and layout features used in letters. Pupils could include an answer to Hannah's question about the cast, and information about when Steph will be back at school.

- Ask pupils if they have ever hurt themselves. What happened? How did they feel? Write a list of the feelings pupils suggest on the board. Ask a volunteer to come to the front of the class and mime one of the feelings. Encourage the rest of the class to guess which feeling is being mimed.

A trip to the shop / No teacher

A trip to the shop

Dad and Freddy went to the shop.

Freddy enjoys going to the shop because he gets to ride in the trolley.

They bought some bread, some milk, some cheese and a box of cereal.

Freddy's stomach rumbled and he said he was going to make a sandwich for lunch.

1 Who did Freddy go to the shop with?
He went with his dad.

2 Why does Freddy like going to the shop?
Because he gets to ride in the trolley.

3 How can you tell that Freddy was hungry?
Because his stomach rumbled and he said he was
going to make a sandwich for lunch.

4 What kind of sandwich do you think Freddy will make?
Think about what Dad and Freddy bought from the shop.
I think he will make a cheese sandwich.

Did you answer all the questions?

@ Not to be photocopied · Year 2 — Targeted Comprehension

A trip to the shop — Page 7

If pupils are struggling with question 3, ask them how they know when they are hungry. What happens to them?

Extra Questions & Activities

- Ask pupils to draw a picture of their favourite sandwich. Ask them to write a shopping list of everything they would need to make it.

- As a class, create a set of instructions for making a cheese sandwich. Encourage pupils to think about how to make the instructions clear so that it would be easy for someone else to follow them. Pupils could make sandwiches by following each other's instructions.

- Write some bullet points on the board about a trip to the shops, mixing up the sentences so that they are in the wrong order. Ask pupils to copy down the bullet points, re-ordering them so that they make sense. Pupils could draw a picture to represent each bullet point.

No teacher

Today, our teacher was off ill and nobody came to teach us. Normally, we have maths on Monday mornings, but instead we played in the home corner. After break time, we usually have science, but today we painted pictures instead. Every day, we have one hour for lunch, but today nobody told us to go back to our lessons. We played outside until home time — it was fantastic!

1 Why didn't the children have a teacher today?
Because their teacher was ill.

2 What do the children usually study on Monday mornings?
maths and science

3 What does the word "fantastic" mean?
E.g. It means really good.

4 Why do you think the children didn't tell anyone that their teacher hadn't come?
E.g. Because they wanted to do fun things like playing
and painting instead of their usual lessons.

Did you answer all the questions?

Year 2 — Targeted Comprehension · @ Not to be photocopied

No teacher — Page 8

Begin by asking pupils about their school routine. Do they know what time school starts and ends?

Extra Questions & Activities

- Ask pupils to imagine that a substitute teacher arrives while the children in the text are painting. What might happen next? How might it change the text? Would the teacher be angry that they have been painting instead of learning science? Or would the teacher join in the fun?

- Discuss pupils' answers to question 3. Can pupils think of any other adjectives that have a similar meaning? Create a list of their suggestions on the board. Ask them to choose one of the words and write a sentence about their favourite subject — e.g. Drama is amazing because I like the games that we play.

- Use the previous activity as a starting point for pupils to create a timetable for their ideal day at school. It may be useful to hand out templates for pupils to fill in. Discuss pupils' timetables as a class — does everybody enjoy the same subjects? Which are the most popular?

The Enchanted Wood / Amy Johnson

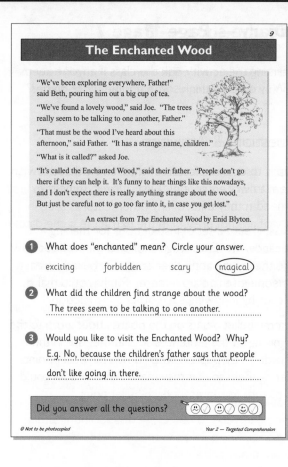

9

The Enchanted Wood

"We've been exploring everywhere, Father!" said Beth, pouring him out a big cup of tea.

"We've found a lovely wood," said Joe. "The trees really seem to be talking to one another, Father."

"That must be the wood I've heard about this afternoon," said Father. "It has a strange name, children."

"What is it called?" asked Joe.

"It's called the Enchanted Wood," said their father. "People don't go there if they can help it. It's funny to hear things like this nowadays, and I don't expect there is really anything strange about the wood. But just be careful not to go too far into it, in case you get lost."

An extract from *The Enchanted Wood* by Enid Blyton.

1 What does "enchanted" mean? Circle your answer.

exciting   forbidden   scary   (magical)

2 What did the children find strange about the wood?
The trees seem to be talking to one another.

3 Would you like to visit the Enchanted Wood? Why?
E.g. No, because the children's father says that people don't like going in there.

Did you answer all the questions? 😕 😐 🙂

© Not to be photocopied   Year 2 — Targeted Comprehension

The Enchanted Wood — Page 9

Before reading the extract, ensure that pupils understand the purpose of speech marks and can recognise when someone is speaking within a text.

Extra Questions & Activities

- Ask pupils if they would like to read the rest of the story. Why or why not? Ask them to write some sentences explaining their answer.

- Ask pupils to discuss the kinds of things that might live in the Enchanted Wood. What would the creatures look like? How might they behave? Ask them to think of some descriptive words and write them on the board. Get pupils to write some sentences describing one creature that might live in the wood using some of the vocabulary from the board.

- Ask pupils to plan a story set in the Enchanted Wood. Encourage them to use bullet points to briefly plan the beginning, middle and end of their stories. Then ask pupils to swap and discuss their ideas with a partner.

- Ask pupils to draw a picture of the Enchanted Wood.

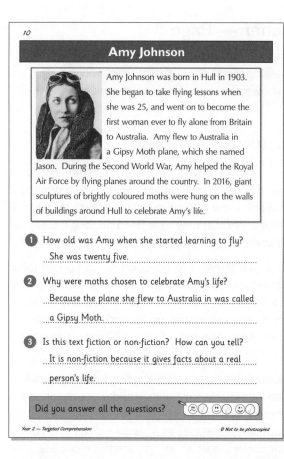

10

Amy Johnson

Amy Johnson was born in Hull in 1903. She began to take flying lessons when she was 25, and went on to become the first woman ever to fly alone from Britain to Australia. Amy flew to Australia in a Gipsy Moth plane, which she named Jason. During the Second World War, Amy helped the Royal Air Force by flying planes around the country. In 2016, giant sculptures of brightly coloured moths were hung on the walls of buildings around Hull to celebrate Amy's life.

1 How old was Amy when she started learning to fly?
She was twenty five.

2 Why were moths chosen to celebrate Amy's life?
Because the plane she flew to Australia in was called a Gipsy Moth.

3 Is this text fiction or non-fiction? How can you tell?
It is non-fiction because it gives facts about a real person's life.

Did you answer all the questions? 😕 😐 🙂

Year 2 — Targeted Comprehension   © Not to be photocopied

Amy Johnson — Page 10

When marking answers to question 2, don't accept answers that just refer to moths being flying animals.

Extra Questions & Activities

- Ask pupils why there are so many words in the extract that start with a capital letter. Remind them of the difference between common and proper nouns. Ask pupils to copy down all the examples of proper nouns from the passage.

- Ask pupils to write down five questions they would like to ask Amy about her life and achievements.

- Show pupils some photos of the moth sculptures mentioned in the text. Ask pupils to create their own designs inspired by what they have learnt about Amy.

- Ask pupils to create a biographical fact sheet about themselves. They should include their birthday, how old they are and where they were born. Pupils could also write a sentence about what they would like to be when they are older and draw a picture of themselves.

Tim's Diary / Plum

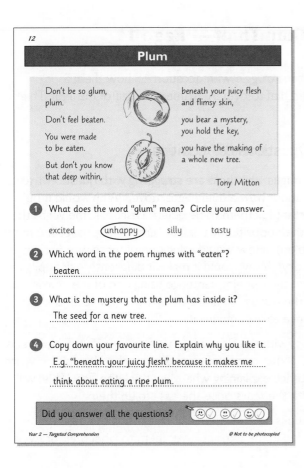

11

Tim's Diary

Dear Diary,

Today, the weather was stormy so we couldn't go outside to play. We thought that the sun might come out this afternoon but it carried on raining. I really wanted to have a picnic in the garden but it was too wet, so Dad built a den in the kitchen to cheer me up. He used lots of blankets and pillows and it was very cosy. We ate a picnic inside the den. It was so yummy — we had jam sandwiches and crisps.

After that, we played a board game, and then we played in the den again until it was bath time.

Now I am tired. I will write to you again tomorrow.

1 How do you think Tim felt when he couldn't have a picnic outside? Tick two options.

☐ happy   ☑ sad   ☑ disappointed   ☐ excited

2 Copy a word from the text that means the same as "tasty".

yummy

3 What do you think Tim did after writing in his diary? How can you tell?

E.g. I think he went to bed because Tim writes that he

is tired.

Did you answer all the questions?

© Not to be photocopied   Year 2 — Targeted Comprehension

Tim's Diary — Page 11

Before starting the activity, ask the class if anyone keeps a diary. Why do they think some people write diaries?

Extra Questions & Activities

- As a class, discuss the features which show that this extract is a diary entry (e.g. "Dear Diary", written in first person). Can they think of any other features used in diaries that are not present in the extract (e.g. the date)?

- Ask pupils to write their own short diary entry about something they did at the weekend. Encourage them to include some of the diary features you have discussed.

- Ask pupils to make a list of other fun activities they could do on a rainy day. Ask them to discuss their work with a partner — are their ideas similar or different? What is their favourite thing to do when it is raining?

- Discuss pupils' answers to question 1, and talk about how pupils react when they feel disappointed. Explore good and bad ways to react to a disappointing situation (e.g. trying to find a solution to the problem compared to being grumpy and shouting).

12

Plum

Don't be so glum, plum.

Don't feel beaten.

You were made to be eaten.

But don't you know that deep within,

beneath your juicy flesh and flimsy skin,

you bear a mystery, you hold the key,

you have the making of a whole new tree.

Tony Mitton

1 What does the word "glum" mean? Circle your answer.

excited   (unhappy)   silly   tasty

2 Which word in the poem rhymes with "eaten"?

beaten

3 What is the mystery that the plum has inside it?

The seed for a new tree.

4 Copy down your favourite line. Explain why you like it.

E.g. "beneath your juicy flesh" because it makes me

think about eating a ripe plum.

Did you answer all the questions?

Year 2 — Targeted Comprehension   © Not to be photocopied

Plum — Page 12

Before reading the poem, ask pupils to look at the picture of the plums on the page. Ensure they understand that the pit or stone is a seed that can grow into a plum tree.

Extra Questions & Activities

- Discuss pupils' answers to question 1. Ask them about the meaning of the prefix 'un'. Can they think of any other words that have a similar meaning to "unhappy"? Ask pupils to think about why it is important to use a variety of adjectives in their writing.

- Ask pupils to identify the words that rhyme in the poem by underlining them in different colours. Can they think of any more words that rhyme with the examples from the poem? Make a list on the board.

- Ask pupils to share their answers to question 4 with the class. Encourage them to think about speaking clearly and listening respectfully when others are speaking.

- Divide pupils into small groups and assign each group a food. Ask them to write a short poem about it. Pupils could draw their food and write their poem inside it.

Making a bird feeder / The Tear Thief

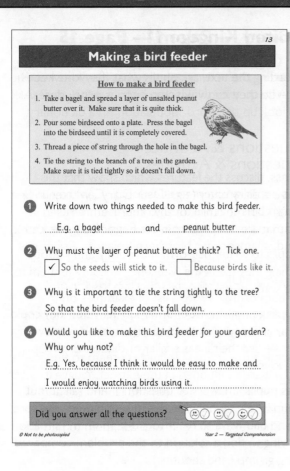

Making a bird feeder — Page 13

Before reading the text, make sure that pupils know that a bagel is a type of bread roll with a hole in the middle.

Extra Questions & Activities

- Discuss with the class why birds might use feeders more often in the winter. Why is it important to feed birds?

- Ask pupils whether they found the instructions easy to follow. Would they change or add anything (e.g. a list of equipment, photos of different stages)? Pupils could follow the instructions to make their own bird feeder.

- Ask pupils to imagine that they have seen a beautiful bird using a feeder in the playground. Ask them to write some bullet points describing the bird. They could draw a picture and label the bird's features.

- As a class, discuss the things that birds eat and make a list on the board (e.g. worms, bread crumbs, seeds). Split pupils into groups and ask them to create a dish for birds using some of the items from the board. Encourage them to think of an inventive name for their dish and draw a picture of it.

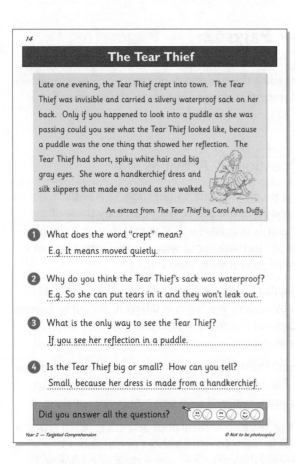

The Tear Thief — Page 14

If children struggle with question 4, show them a handkerchief to help them infer the size of the Tear Thief.

Extra Questions & Activities

- Encourage pupils who are struggling with question 1 to think about how a thief might move. Why would it be important for them to be quiet? Discuss some verbs that have the opposite meaning to "crept" (e.g. barged, burst, stumbled). How would using one of these words change the story? Why would it make it different? Ask pupils to rewrite the opening sentence using one of the words from the discussion and then write a new second sentence to accompany it.

- Discuss with the class why they think the Tear Thief steals tears. What does she want them for? Ask pupils to write a sentence explaining what they think the Tear Thief will do with the tears once she has stolen them.

- Ask pupils to draw the Tear Thief using the description provided in the extract. Ask them to label their drawing.

The United Kingdom / Our Solar System

15

The United Kingdom

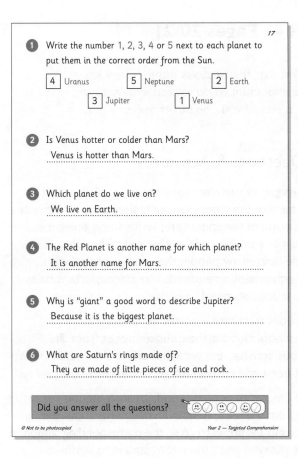

UK stands for United Kingdom. There are four countries in the UK — Northern Ireland, Scotland, Wales and England. The UK's flag is called the Union Jack.

The capital of Northern Ireland is Belfast. The Irish Sea separates Northern Ireland from the rest of the UK.

Scotland's capital is Edinburgh. Scotland includes over seven hundred islands. Most of the islands don't have any people living on them.

Cardiff is the capital of Wales. Leeks and daffodils are symbols of Wales. People wear them on their clothes on St David's day.

England's capital city is London. England is the largest country in the UK and has the biggest population.

1 Why can't you walk from Northern Ireland to England?
Because the Irish Sea is in the way.

2 Which UK country includes over seven hundred islands?
Scotland

3 Write the names of two plants that are symbols of Wales.
leeks and daffodils

4 Which country in the UK has the most people living there?
England

Did you answer all the questions? ☺☺ ☺☺ ☺☺

© Not to be photocopied   Year 2 — Targeted Comprehension

The United Kingdom — Page 15

Before reading the text, ask pupils what they know about the UK — do they know which countries it includes? Ask pupils to look up the word "population" in a dictionary.

Extra Questions & Activities

- Discuss pupils' answers to question 3. Can they think of any symbols that are used to represent other countries in the UK (e.g. rose for England, thistle for Scotland, shamrock for Northern Ireland). Ask pupils to think of something that is considered typical of each country in the UK (e.g. fish and chips, haggis, soda bread, bara brith). Write a list of examples on the board. Ask pupils to use these examples as a starting point for creating a leaflet about the UK.

- Give pupils a map of the UK and ask them to find the places that are mentioned in the extract. Suggest some other well-known places and landmarks and ask them to find these too (e.g. the River Thames, the English Channel). You could also ask them to find the region or town where they live.

17

1 Write the number 1, 2, 3, 4 or 5 next to each planet to put them in the correct order from the Sun.

4 Uranus   5 Neptune   2 Earth
3 Jupiter   1 Venus

2 Is Venus hotter or colder than Mars?
Venus is hotter than Mars.

3 Which planet do we live on?
We live on Earth.

4 The Red Planet is another name for which planet?
It is another name for Mars.

5 Why is "giant" a good word to describe Jupiter?
Because it is the biggest planet.

6 What are Saturn's rings made of?
They are made of little pieces of ice and rock.

Did you answer all the questions? ☺☺ ☺☺ ☺☺

© Not to be photocopied   Year 2 — Targeted Comprehension

Our Solar System — Pages 16-17

Before starting the activity, explore pupils' knowledge of the planets. Do they know any of their names?

Extra Questions & Activities

- Discuss pupils' answers to question 4. Ask pupils to think of ways to describe the other planets using the information from the text. Encourage them to be as creative as possible (e.g. Jupiter shouldn't be the Big Planet, it could be the Enormous or Vast Planet).

- Ask pupils why they think Earth is the only planet that humans live on. As a class, discuss the things humans need in order to survive (e.g. water, food, air to breathe, a suitable temperature). Explain that Earth is the only planet in the solar system that provides for all these needs. Ask pupils what they might need to survive on Mars (e.g. tanks of oxygen, heated spacesuits).

- Ask pupils to imagine what it would be like to visit another planet. Get them to write a description of the experience. They could include the journey, their first impressions and what they found when they explored.

On the farm / Sports

1 Put a tick in each row to show which child is wearing which item of clothing.

	Andy	Josh	Susan	Rachel
red boots				✓
blue overalls	✓			
orange hat		✓		
purple overalls			✓	

2 What is Andy going to do next?
He is going to dig up the cabbages.

3 Why do you think Josh is putting the strawberries into the bowl carefully?
So he doesn't squash them.

4 What is Susan doing?
She is feeding the animals.

5 Why are Susan and Andy wearing overalls?
So that their clothes don't get dirty.

6 Why has Rachel brought a basket?
So that she can collect eggs from the hens.

Did you answer all the questions?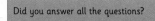

© Not to be photocopied   Year 2 — Targeted Comprehension

On the farm — Pages 18-19

If pupils are struggling, discuss the text with them and ask them to identify each character in the picture.

Extra Questions & Activities

- Pupils could use the information in the text to colour in the picture in the Question Book.

- Ask pupils to circle the animals in the picture and then write the names of the animals on the board. Do pupils know why each animal is useful (e.g. we get wool from sheep, eggs from hens and milk from cows)?

- Give each pupil a picture of an item of food (e.g. omelette, cheese, flour). Ask them to think about what it's made from. Write categories such as eggs, milk and plants on the board, and ask pupils to put their food under the correct category.

- Ask pupils to write a short text in a similar style to the extract, describing themselves and some friends in the playground. They could then swap their text with a partner and try to draw what their partner has written.

---

1 Why is it important to do exercise?
So that you stay healthy.

2 In football, how many people on each team are allowed to pick up the ball?
One person on each team is allowed to pick up the ball.

3 Table tennis uses a shuttlecock. Is this true or false?
False

4 Judo is a martial art. Explain what this means.
It is a sport that involves self-defence.

5 Which sport is played by the largest team?
Football is played by the largest team.

6 Which do you think would be the hardest sport? Why?
E.g. Judo, because you have to be very strong.

7 Do you like to play sports? Which one is your favourite?
E.g. Yes. My favourite sport is rugby.

Did you answer all the questions?

© Not to be photocopied   Year 2 — Targeted Comprehension

Sports — Pages 20-21

Before reading the text, ask pupils if they know why it is important to do exercise. What can happen to you if you don't exercise enough?

Extra Questions & Activities

- Discuss pupils' answers to question 7. Write a list on the board of the different sports they play. Ask pupils to pick one of the sports and write some sentences about it in a similar style to the text. They should include how many people the sport is played with, what equipment is required, and any important rules that participants need to know.

- Ask pupils to create a poster advertising an after-school club for their chosen sport from the previous activity. Encourage them to think about what might persuade children to go to the club.

- In the classroom or playground, create a 'station' for each sport from the text. Read out statements about the sports and ask pupils to go to the corresponding station. Ask pupils who go to the wrong station to sit down.

Habitats / Flat Stanley

1. Why do you think it is difficult for animals to live in desert habitats?
   Because it is very dry and there aren't many plants.

2. What is the biggest tropical rainforest in the world?
   The Amazon is the biggest tropical rainforest.

3. Give one difference between a desert and a rainforest.
   A desert doesn't get a lot of rain but a rainforest does.

4. What is an ocean?
   It is a large area of salt water.

5. Name two animals that live in an ocean habitat.
   E.g. dolphins   and   turtles

6. What type of habitat is the city of London?
   It is an urban habitat.

7. Can you think of another wild animal that has learnt to live in an urban habitat?
   E.g. Foxes

Did you answer all the questions?

© Not to be photocopied   Year 2 — Targeted Comprehension

Habitats — Pages 22-23

If pupils are struggling with question 1, encourage them to think about the things animals need to survive. How do they know there isn't much water in the desert?

Extra Questions & Activities

- Ask pupils if this text is fiction or non-fiction. Make a list of non-fiction features and ask pupils to label the ones that are present in the text.

- As a class, discuss another habitat that is not mentioned in the extract (e.g. woodland). Write facts about the habitat on the board. Ask pupils to write a paragraph about this habitat in a similar style to the extract.

- Discuss pupils' answers to question 7 and write their suggestions on the board. Why did pupils pick each animal — have they seen them near their homes?

- Show pupils pictures of the habitats mentioned in the extract. Ask them to identify the key features of each habitat and discuss the types of animals that might live there. Ask pupils to design an imaginary animal with features suitable for it to live in a pond.

1. At what time of day is the text set? How do you know?
   E.g. The morning because they're about to eat breakfast.

2. Is Stanley older or younger than Arthur?
   He is older than Arthur.

3. Why do you think the author uses exclamation marks when Arthur says "Hey! Come and look! Hey!"?
   E.g. To show that Arthur is shouting.

4. Why does Mr. Lambchop tell Arthur "Hay is for horses"?
   E.g. Because he thinks it was impolite for Arthur to shout "Hey". The words "hay" and "hey" sound the same.

5. What woke Stanley up?
   Arthur's shouting woke him up.

6. Copy a word from the text that shows Stanley isn't worried about being under the board.
   cheerfully

Did you answer all the questions?

© Not to be photocopied   Year 2 — Targeted Comprehension

Flat Stanley — Pages 24-25

Flat Stanley is an American book and so contains American spellings, such as "favor". You may want to point these out to children so they don't get confused.

Extra Questions & Activities

- Ask pupils to identify whether this is a fiction or non-fiction text. How do they know?

- Discuss pupils' answers to question 3. How do the exclamation marks affect the way you read the text? Write some sentences on the board and ask pupils to decide whether they need an exclamation mark, a question mark or a full stop.

- Divide the class into groups of four and ask them to act out the scene. Encourage them to think carefully about how the characters might be feeling and how they could express these emotions.

- Ask pupils to imagine that they are Stanley. Ask them to write a diary entry about waking up under the bulletin board. They should include what they could see and what they thought was happening.

Animals / Slippers at school?

27

1 Which group of animals only eats plants?
Herbivores only eat plants.

2 Why do frogs have strong legs?
So that they can jump.

3 How can you tell that snakes are carnivores?
Because they eat mice.

4 Why do bats need to have very good hearing?
So that they can find insects to eat in the dark.

5 Can all birds fly? Explain how you know this from the text.
No. The text says ostriches are birds but they can't fly.

6 What does the word "unique" mean?
It means something that's not the same as anything else.

7 Give one example of a mammal from the text.
What makes an animal a mammal?
E.g. Zebra. An animal is a mammal if it makes milk
for its babies.

Did you answer all the questions?

© Not to be photocopied   Year 2 — Targeted Comprehension

Animals — Pages 26-27

It may be useful to recap what pupils know about animal classification before they read this text.

Extra Questions & Activities

- Discuss the meaning of the words "nocturnal" and "diurnal" with the class. Ask pupils to split a page into two columns. They should write "active at night" at the top of one column and "active during the day" at the top of the other. Ask them to think of three animals for each column.

- Ask pupils to think of an animal that they are familiar with. Get them to write a paragraph about it in a similar style to the text. They could also draw a picture of their animal.

- Write the categories 'mammal', 'reptile', 'bird', 'amphibian' and 'fish' on the board. As a class, discuss the qualities that animals in each category have. Hand out pictures of different animals to pupils, and ask them to identify which category they belong to.

29

1 Why do the teachers want the children to wear slippers?
Tick one.
☐ Because the children move more quietly in slippers.
☑ Because research showed that it could improve their grades.
☐ Because the children kept getting cold feet in the classroom.

2 The teachers "pitched the idea" to the pupils.
What do you think this means?
E.g. It means they asked pupils if they liked the idea.

3 Copy the sentence that describes what has changed at the school since slippers were allowed.
There is less stomping around and children are calmer
and more relaxed.

4 How do the children in the article feel about wearing slippers to school?
They really like it.

5 Would you like to wear slippers at school? Why or why not?
E.g. Yes, because slippers are comfortable and it would
make me feel more relaxed at school.

Did you answer all the questions?

© Not to be photocopied   Year 2 — Targeted Comprehension

Slippers at school? — Pages 28-29

Before reading the extract, explain to the class that the extract is from a newspaper article. Ask them to look at the extract and discuss the purpose of the headline.

Extra Questions & Activities

- Discuss pupils' answers to question 6. How many pupils would like to wear slippers and how many would not? Is the class split evenly or is one view more popular? Ask pupils to explain their arguments and present a case for or against slippers being worn at their school.

- Split the class into small groups and ask pupils to plan a presentation to "pitch the idea" of wearing slippers in school to the head teacher. Encourage pupils to think about which arguments are most likely to persuade the head teacher to support the idea.

- Ask pupils to draw and label the perfect pair of slippers to wear at school. They should include sentences to explain each feature (e.g. fluffy insides to keep my feet warm, grips on the soles so I don't slip).

The Selfish Giant / The Monkeys and the Crocodile

1 Find and copy two adjectives which describe the grass in the Giant's garden.

............soft............ and ....green..........

2 What do you think "furiously" means?

E.g. very angrily

3 Write down a word to describe how the children felt when they left the garden. Explain your answer.

E.g. Sad, because they weren't allowed to play in the garden and they didn't have anywhere else to play.

4 Why is the Giant described as "selfish"?

E.g. Because he wants to keep the garden all to himself.

5 What does this story teach us about being selfish?

E.g. If you share something then you can enjoy it more than if you are selfish and keep it to yourself.

6 Did you like this story? Why or why not?

E.g. Yes, because I like the ending when the children go back into the garden and spring comes.

Did you answer all the questions?

The Selfish Giant — Pages 30-31

Before reading the text, it may be helpful to check pupils' understanding of the word "selfish".

Extra Questions & Activities

- Ask pupils to think about how the Giant reacted when he found the children in his garden. How could the Giant have reacted differently? How might it change the rest of the story if the Giant didn't get angry with the children?

- As a class, make a list of the words pupils suggested in their answers to question 3. Then, ask pupils to think of words to describe how the children felt when they were playing in the garden. Discuss the differences between the two lists. Encourage pupils to think about how their actions can make other people feel.

- Ask pupils to design a garden that they would enjoy playing in. Would it have lots of trees or flowers? What play equipment would it have? Ask pupils to draw a labelled diagram of their garden. Encourage them to explain why they have included each feature.

1 Which word in this poem rhymes with "right"?

bite

2 The monkeys tell the crocodile to "Come and take a bite!" Do you think they mean it? Explain your answer.

E.g. No, because they are teasing the crocodile. They don't really want to get bitten by the crocodile.

3 Find a word from the text that means the same as "crying".

weeping

4 What happens to the monkeys' brother?

He gets eaten by the crocodile.

5 How do the monkeys' feelings change in the poem?

E.g. At the start of the poem the monkeys are happy and excited. At the end they are sad.

6 Do you think the monkeys got what they deserved? Why or why not?

E.g. No, because no one deserves to be eaten by a crocodile.

Did you answer all the questions?

The Monkeys and the Crocodile — Pages 32-33

Ask pupils what they think "merry" and "dreary" mean. They can check their answers in a dictionary.

Extra Questions & Activities

- Ask pupils to identify rhyming words within the poem, and look at the rhyming pairs "right" and "bite", and "air" and "care". What do pupils notice about the spelling of the rhyming words? Ask them to think of other words that are spelt differently but also rhyme.

- As a class, look at the poem's rhyming pattern. What is the poem's rhyme scheme?

- Discuss with pupils how the crocodile feels during the poem. Is he upset by the monkeys teasing him? Or is he just waiting for his opportunity to strike? Write a short story describing the crocodile's version of events.

- Explain to pupils that this poem has a moral — do they know what the moral is? Can they think of any other stories or poems that have a moral?

The Hundred-Mile-An-Hour Dog

Question Book:
Year 3 Ready, pages 2-3

Author / Source:
Jeremy Strong

Genre:
Fiction — novel extract

Cross-curricular links:
* Drama (expressions)
* Art (comic strip)

Introduction

Jeremy Strong is a prolific English author who has written over 100 children's books. In *The Hundred-Mile-An-Hour Dog,* a boy called Trevor attempts to train his dog, Streaker, during the school holidays. This proves to be much more difficult than first expected, as Streaker likes to go fast, leaving Trevor and his friend Tina struggling to keep up. Their various attempts to keep Streaker under control land them in lots of trouble, especially with bully Charlie Smugg and his dad, the police officer Sergeant Smugg. In this extract, Tina is using her bike to pull along a bowl of dog food for Streaker to chase. But events take a turn for the worse when Sergeant Smugg arrives on the scene.

Answers

1. Any two from: raced; whizzing; hurtled; charging; pounding; zoomed.

2. Any appropriate answer. E.g. No. Because it shows you how much Streaker wanted the food in the bowl.

3. E.g. The police siren and Sergeant Smugg shouting.

4. E.g. She was really scared.

5. Streaker was eating noisily.

6. a noun

7. Any appropriate answer. E.g. It crashed into a hedge and a ditch. The radiator was damaged.

Extra Activities

* Talk through the extract with the class. How many characters are present, and what are their names? Can pupils summarise what happens in the extract? Ask pupils to write a paragraph describing what they think might happen next.

* Explain to the class that the police officer, Sergeant Smugg, isn't very nice. How might the extract have been different if the police officer was friendly?

* Ask pupils to make a list of words or phrases to describe how Sergeant Smugg might be feeling at the end of the extract. Encourage pupils to share some of their ideas and explain why they chose them.

* Ask pupils to consider the name Streaker. As a class, discuss why she might have been given this name. Get pupils to think of other appropriate names for a really fast dog.

* In small groups, ask pupils to discuss how Trevor's feelings change throughout this extract. Encourage pupils to mime his different feelings, using facial expressions rather than words to express his reactions.

* Ask the class if anyone has a pet at home. Have their pets ever done anything that has got them into trouble? Ask the children to draw a comic strip about a naughty pet that causes problems for its owner.

The Painting Lesson

Question Book:
Year 3 Ready, pages 4-5

Author / Source:
Trevor Harvey

Genre:
Poetry

Cross-curricular links:
* Art (drawing)
* PSHE (difference; bullying)

Introduction

Trevor Harvey is a British poet who writes comic poems for children, as well as short sketches and plays. His poem 'The Painting Lesson' adds a comic twist to a typical encounter between teacher and pupil during an art lesson. The teacher chastises the child for their thoughtless depiction of mummy with splodges and garish colours, but has a shock when the child's mother arrives at the end of the day looking exactly like the child's painting. This poem provides an excellent opportunity to open up discussion with pupils about difference and tolerance.

Answers

1. Trevor Harvey

2. E.g. Because she doesn't think it looks like the child's mum.

3. Any pair from: replied and tried; know and go; smile and while; pink and think; three and me.

4. E.g. He puts them in capitals. It makes you say them louder.

5. Any appropriate answer. E.g. Embarrassed because she thought the child hadn't tried on the first picture, but it actually looked just like the child's mum.

6. Any appropriate answer. E.g. Yes, because it was funny that the teacher was wrong and the mum really was an orange and green blob.

Extra Activities

* Ask pupils to share their answers to question 6 in the Question Book. Were they surprised by the ending of the poem? Did they think it was funny? Why?

* As a class, discuss pupils' answers to question 4. Ask them to read the poem aloud, emphasising the words in capitals. Can they think of other ways to emphasise words in a text (e.g. italics, underlining)?

* Ask pupils to identify pairs of lines within the poem that rhyme. As a class, work out whether the poem has a regular or an irregular rhyme scheme. Ask pupils to write their own poem about their favourite subject. They could use an irregular rhyme scheme or follow the same rhyming pattern as the penultimate verse of the poem (ABCB).

* Ask pupils to draw the child's mum, and then draw a similar picture to the one the teacher helped with. Ask them to write some sentences explaining the similarities and differences between the two.

* Talk to students about the fact that the child's mum is different to what the teacher expected. Is she different to the children's own parents? Discuss why it is important for people to be different. Ask children to explain how they think they should treat people who are different to themselves and why.

* Ask pupils if they have ever been treated badly because of something that makes them different. How did it make them feel? As a class, think of some messages to make everyone feel welcome and valued. Ask pupils to write and colour these messages and display them around the room.

Fossil Hunting

Question Book:
Year 3 Ready, pages 6-7

Author / Source:
www.ordnancesurvey.co.uk

Genre:
Non-fiction — reference text

Cross-curricular links:
- History (dinosaurs)
- Geography (tides)

Introduction

Fossils are remains or traces of prehistoric life, often preserved in rock. Detailed study of the fossil record has contributed to our understanding of life before recorded history, providing evidence of evolution and allowing us to learn about extinct plants, animals and other organisms. As conditions for fossilisation are ideal on the sea floor, many fossils are marine, and they often wash up on beaches. Fossils can be found all over Britain, but some of the most famous areas for fossil hunting are the 'Jurassic Coast' of east Devon and Dorset, the Isle of Wight and the east coast of Yorkshire. Before reading the extract with the class, ensure that pupils have a basic understanding of what fossils are.

Answers

1. observant

2. false

3. E.g. So that they don't break when you put sharp or heavy rocks and fossils in them.

4. delicate

5. E.g. So that an expert can look at it and tell you if it is an important scientific find.

6. E.g. To make the list of equipment stand out from the rest of the text.
   It also helps to make the list easier to read.

7. Any appropriate answer. E.g. Yes, because it would be fun to go to a beach and look for fossils. I would be really excited if I found a fossil and I would enjoy taking it to a heritage centre to learn more about it.

Extra Activities

- Ask pupils to imagine that an important new fossil has been discovered. Get them to write a newspaper article about the discovery. They could include where the fossil was found, who found it, a description of the discovery and what is going to happen to the fossil next.

- This extract is taken from a beginners' guide to fossil hunting. Ask pupils to write a beginners' guide for their favourite hobby or sport. Where and when could a beginner try the activity? What equipment would they need? Encourage pupils to include some 'top tips' to help a beginner get started.

- Explain to the class that almost all our information about dinosaurs comes from fossils. Ask pupils if they know the names of any dinosaurs, and then assign a dinosaur to each child. Ask them to research their dinosaur and create a poster describing it. How big was it? What did it eat? What did it look like? Pupils could include an illustration of their dinosaur.

  Stegosaurus
  Triceratops
  Apatosaurus
  Alamosaurus
  Velociraptor
  Brachiosaurus
  Diplodocus

- Ask pupils about high and low tides. Ask them to think about why it might be dangerous to go on the beach at high tide. Discuss why it is important to research high tides and take safety seriously when planning a fossil hunting trip.

Enid Blyton and the Secret Seven

Question Book:
Year 3 Ready, pages 8-9

Author / Source:
Gillian Baverstock

Genre:
Non-fiction — letter

Cross-curricular links:
*   D&T (designing a secret den)
*   History (changes within living memory)

Introduction

Enid Blyton was born in 1897 and went on to become a famous children's author, writing hundreds of books. Her popularity has continued since her death in 1968, and many of her stories have been adapted for television or the theatre, including *Noddy* and *The Famous Five*. Her daughter, Gillian Baverstock, also became a writer, and has written and talked extensively about her mother's life and works. In this letter, Gillian explains how her mother came to write one of her most popular series, *The Secret Seven*. Before pupils read the text, ask them if they have read any of Enid Blyton's books. Which ones? Did they enjoy them?

Answers

1. a shed

2. a. a letter
    b. E.g. Because it starts with "Dear" and ends with "from".

3. E.g. Because she wanted to find out more about his secret society.

4. Any appropriate answer. E.g. Pleased because he had been hoping that Enid Blyton would write about him and his friends.

5. E.g. Yes, because lots of children asked Enid to write another, longer story about them.

6. Any appropriate answer. E.g. I would be excited because they could tell me about the adventures that they used to have.

Extra Activities

*   Ask pupils to write a letter from Enid Blyton to Peter. What questions might she have wanted to ask him about his secret society? Before they start, remind them of the layout features of a formal letter.

*   Ask pupils to imagine that they have been sent some money to buy a feast for their friends. Get them to write a paragraph describing the food that they would buy.

*   Explain to pupils that Enid Blyton also wrote a series called *The Famous Five*. Can pupils think of adjectives that could be used to describe other numbers? E.g. Exciting Eight, Troublesome Two, Super Six. Ask them to write their own adventure story involving one of the groups they have invented.

*   Ask pupils to imagine that they and their friends have formed a secret society. Where would they have their secret meeting place? What would it be like? Ask them to draw and label a diagram of their secret den, then discuss their design with a partner. Encourage them to explain the reasons behind each aspect of their design.

*   Ask the children to think about the fact that the original Secret Seven are now grandparents. How do pupils think the world has changed since their grandparents were children? What are the differences between the time when their grandparents grew up and now? On the board, create a list with the children of things that were different and things that are still the same.

The Queen's Nose

Question Book:
Year 3 Ready, pages 10-11

Author / Source:
Dick King-Smith

Genre:
Fiction — novel extract

Cross-curricular links:
• Art (drawing)

Introduction

Before becoming a published author at the age of 56, Dick King-Smith worked as a soldier in the Second World War, a farmer and a primary school teacher. *The Queen's Nose* is about a young girl called Harmony who loves animals, but is not allowed any pets. Because of this, she imagines all the people she meets as animals. One day, Harmony receives a magic fifty pence piece from her uncle. She is granted seven wishes by the coin, but they are not always granted in the way that Harmony expects. The book carries an important message to be careful what you wish for.

Answers

1. E.g. No, because she checks that no-one is watching before she makes her wish.

2. E.g. Because he has a pouch, strong legs and a sheeplike face.

3. E.g. Because she thinks a watch will appear.

4. E.g. Because Harmony thinks the postman looks like a kangaroo and kangaroos hop.

5. Any appropriate answer. E.g. Excited. The text says that her hands are trembling.

6. A watch.

7. Any appropriate answer. E.g. Lucky, because she has a magic coin that can make her wishes come true.

Extra Activities

• Ask the students to think about what animal Harmony might compare them to. Ask them to write a description of themselves as that animal.

• Tell pupils that Harmony's magic coin only gives each person seven wishes. Ask them to split a page into seven sections and write down seven things they would wish for. They should explain why they would make each wish and how it might change their life.

• Ask pupils to imagine receiving an exciting parcel in the post. Ask them to draw the parcel, and then write a diary entry about the day they received it. Was it something they were expecting or was it a surprise? How did they feel when they were opening it? What was inside?

• As a class, create a story about 'the wish that went wrong'. Ask pupils to imagine making a wish and it being answered in a different way to what they expected. Once completed, pupils could draw pictures to illustrate the story.

• Ask pupils whether they have ever received anything in the post from another country. Have they ever received something strange in the post? Tell pupils that some visitors to Hawaii send coconuts to their friends instead of sending postcards. The coconuts are painted with bright colours and imaginative designs. Ask students to draw a coconut and then create a design to send to a friend or relative (make sure they remember to include space for the address).

Making an Air Rocket

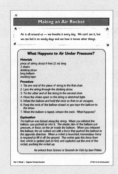

Question Book:
Year 3 Ready, pages 12-13

Author / Source:
Jean Potter

Genre:
Non-fiction — instructional text

Cross-curricular links:
* Science (forces)

Introduction

Jean Potter's *Science in Seconds for Kids* is full of quick and simple experiments designed to inspire children with an enthusiasm for science and encourage them to think more deeply about the world around them. This experiment is taken from the section about air. It helps children to understand how the air around them interacts with other objects. Before reading the text, it may be helpful to ask pupils what they know about air. How can they tell it is all around them, even though they can't see it, taste it or smell it?

Answers

1. E.g. To show what order to do things in.

2. Materials — Things I need
   Procedure — What to do
   Explanation — What it means

3. E.g. Because if you don't hold the neck closed, the air will come out of the balloon.

4. Air was <u>pushed</u> into the balloon when you <u>inflated</u> it. When the balloon was <u>released</u>, the air rushed out of it, pushing it in the opposite direction.

5. E.g. When fuel is set on fire, it explodes out of the rocket. This pushes the rocket off the ground.

Extra Activities

* Ask pupils what type of text this is. What features show that it is an instructional text (e.g. ordered sequencing of steps, imperative verbs, subheadings)? Can they see how much easier it is to follow instructions when they are set out in this way?

* Talk through the experiment with the class. What things do they need to do the experiment? Divide the class into several groups and get pupils to carry out the experiment, following the instructions in the extract. Talk through what happened at the end. Once pupils are confident with what they have to do, have a rocket race to see which group can get their balloon to travel the furthest.

* Ask pupils to think about how successful or unsuccessful the experiment they have just performed was. Did anything go wrong? Were there any instructions that were difficult to follow, or anything they could have improved upon? As a class, re-write the instructions on the board, including any amendments that the class think would make the experiment easier and more successful.

* Remind pupils of the key features of instructional texts. Ask them to write instructions to explain how to wrap a present. Make sure they include a list of things they will need and set out the instructions in a clear, chronological order. You could follow this up by asking them to write another set of instructions of their own choice for a classmate to follow.

Dave Pigeon

Question Book:
Year 3 Ready, pages 14-15

Author / Source:
Swapna Haddow

Genre:
Fiction — novel extract

Cross-curricular links:
- Art (drawing)
- PSHE (pests; caring for the environment)
- Science (food chains)

Introduction

The novel *Dave Pigeon* by children's author Swapna Haddow won the Greenhouse Funny Prize in 2014 and was shortlisted for the Sainsbury's Children's Book Awards in 2016. Written from the perspective of Skipper the pigeon, the book follows Skipper and his friend Dave as they attempt to find food and evade their enemy, Mean Cat. This extract begins on a typical morning but ends in a close encounter with Mean Cat — the first time the pigeons meet this dangerous adversary. Before reading the extract, ask children to read the introduction to the text. What dangers do they think Skipper and Dave might have to face?

Answers

1. bright; sunny

2. E.g. It shows you they are really hungry because they would eat their own feathers.

3. E.g. Because that is the name that Skipper and Dave have given her.

4. E.g. Because they are really hungry.

5. a verb

6. Any appropriate answer. E.g. A cat jumps out from behind the basket and attacks the pigeons.

7. Any appropriate answer. E.g. They will fly away from the cat. The cat will be angry that they got away so it will keep trying to find them.

Extra Activities

- Ask pupils to draw a pigeon feast. Ask them to write a paragraph explaining why they think a pigeon would like the food they have chosen.

- As a class, make a list of other animals you might see in the park. Ask pupils to choose an animal from the list and write a story from its perspective about a morning in the park. How do people treat them? What can they hear, see and smell? What happens when one of the park keepers suddenly tries to catch them?

- Ask pupils what they know about pests. Explain that, although it can be a delight to see wild animals, sometimes these creatures can be pests. As a class, discuss some of the problems that can arise from too many pigeons, seagulls or foxes and the dilemmas that face people who have to deal with them.

- Discuss with the class how Dave and Skipper are surviving off rubbish left by humans. Explain that when animals eat rubbish left by humans, it can hurt them and make them ill. Encourage a discussion about how humans affect animals and the environment. Can pupils think of ways that they can look after nature and minimise their own impact?

- Explain that food chains show what animals eat, and usually start with a plant. Can pupils draw a food chain that includes croissant crumbs, the pigeons and Mean Cat? Can they suggest any other food chains that you might find in a park? Discuss as a class and ask pupils to draw some examples.

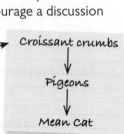

Croissant crumbs
↓
Pigeons
↓
Mean Cat

Cuddly Toys in Space!

Question Book:
Year 3 Ready, pages 16-17

Author / Source:
www.ngkids.co.uk

Genre:
Non-fiction — news article

Cross-curricular links:
- Art (poster)
- D&T (making parachutes)
- Science (space exploration)

Introduction

In 2016, Morecambe Bay Community primary school sent Sam, a cuddly toy dog, into space along with a camera. This was part of a school physics project, which aimed to capture views of Earth from space. For the project, the school collaborated with sentintospace.com, an organisation that works with schools to create engaging projects that encourage an interest in science. Before reading the text, it may be helpful to discuss the words in the glossary with the class and check that pupils are comfortable with their meanings.

Answers

1. E.g. Because they were doing a science project.

2. huge OR much bigger than your average

3. spring

4. E.g. I think that they were excited because they started cheering.

5. E.g. Because it was designed to burst when it got to a certain height.

6. E.g. Slowly. The article says the balloon "drifted" down.

7. E.g. Because they don't know where Sam is and they want to find him.

Extra Activities

- Ask pupils what type of text this is. What features show that it is a newspaper article (e.g. headline, columns)? Do they know any other common newspaper features that are not present in this text?

- Ask pupils to create a poster for the FindSam campaign. Ask them to draw a picture of Sam and write a description of what they think he looks like. They could also include information like where he was last tracked to, who to contact if he is found, and what the reward will be for finding him.

- Ask pupils to write an interview with Sam after his return home. Encourage them to think about what Sam could see during his trip into space, what he might have been feeling, and what he thinks about his adventure now that he has returned safely. Ask some pupils to read out their interviews for the class.

- Ask pupils to predict whether a small parachute would be more or less effective than a large one. Get them to test their predictions by making parachutes from different sized squares cut from plastic bags. They will need to fix a string at each corner and join the strings together with a lump of sticky tac. Test the parachutes by dropping them while standing on a chair. Were their predictions correct?

- As a class, make a list of famous astronauts. Do pupils know why Yuri Gagarin is famous (the first person in space)? What about Neil Armstrong (the first person on the moon)? Assign each child a famous astronaut. Ask them to research their astronaut and create a fact sheet about them. They could include where their astronaut is from and why they are famous.

  > Yuri Gagarin
  > Neil Armstrong
  > Buzz Aldrin
  > Sally Ride
  > John Glenn
  > Mae Jemison
  > Kalpana Chawla

The Baobab Tree

Question Book:
Year 3 Ready, pages 18-19

Author / Source:
Louie Stowell

Genre:
Folk tale

Cross-curricular links:

* PSHE (conflict resolution; healthy eating)

* Geography (continents)

Introduction

Baobab trees grow in mainland Africa, Madagascar and Australia, and can store large amounts of water in their trunks to help them survive in times of drought. The fruit of the Baobab tree is naturally high in vitamin C and calcium, and has even been described as a 'superfood'. The Baobab tree has many thin branches which look like the tree's roots. As a result, it is often referred to as the 'upside down' tree, and its strange appearance has become the source of many folk tales. This engaging extract narrates one of these tales and introduces pupils to a story they may not have heard before. Before reading the extract with the class, make sure they know what a folk tale is. Can they think of any folk tales that they already know?

Answers

1. 1. The gods make the Baobab tree.
    2. The Baobab tree wants to be taller.
    3. The Baobab tree demands to have fruit.

2. E.g. To show that the tree was shouting loudly.

3. E.g. At first they are pleased with the tree but then they get angry with it because it shouts and complains so much.

4. E.g. It is buried upside down in the ground so that it can't speak any more.

5. E.g. Why the Baobab tree looks like it is growing upside down.

Extra Activities

*   Discuss with the class what they thought about the end of the story. Were they surprised by the ending? Do they think the Baobab tree deserved what happened to it? Talk about different ways in which the gods could have resolved their problems with the tree.

*   As a class, make a list of things in nature that could be explained by folk tales (e.g. why zebras have stripes, how giraffes got their long necks, where the rain comes from). Ask pupils to choose an item from the list and write a folk tale to explain it.

*   Tell pupils that the Baobab tree produces fruit. Show them some pictures and ask them to imagine what they think it would taste like. Inform pupils that some African communities are trying to develop international trade in the Baobab fruit. Ask them to make posters to promote the fruit.

*   As a class, make a list of 'superfoods' (e.g. blueberries, kale, seaweed). Assign each child a superfood. Ask them to research it and create a fact sheet about it. They could include a recipe that uses their superfood.

*   Explain that the Baobab tree grows in Africa and Australia. Can pupils find these continents on a map? Write a heading on the board for each continent, then name different countries and ask pupils which continent they belong to (e.g. Egypt, New Zealand). Split the class into groups and assign each group a country to research. They should find their country on a map, then find out the name of its capital city and the main language(s) spoken there. Ask pupils to share their findings with the class.

Excuses, Excuses, Excuses

Question Book:
Year 3 Ready, pages 20-21

Author / Source:
Roger McGough

Genre:
Poetry

Cross-curricular links:
• Art (comic strip)

Introduction

Roger McGough is a famous English poet. He was born on the outskirts of Liverpool in 1937 and became an important member of the Liverpool Poets group in his youth. He writes poetry for both adults and children, and has published over 50 books. 'Excuses, Excuses, Excuses' is an engaging and witty poem that will appeal to pupils of this age group. Before reading the poem with the class, get them to read the title and introduction. What do they think the poem is going to be about? What kind of excuses are they expecting? Encourage them to discuss their ideas with a partner.

Answers

1. flooded and shuddered

2. 1. Dogs were chased by foxes.
   2. A zebra crossing ran away.
   3. Cars ate bikes.

3. the past tense

4. four

5. fly

6. Any appropriate answer. E.g. No, because lots of the things that happen in the poem are impossible. Lamp posts and traffic lights can't move, and trees don't have knees.

Extra Activities

• Ask pupils to share their answers to question 1. Explain that words that almost rhyme are known as half rhymes. Can they think of half rhymes for any other words within the poem?

• Ask students to write a response to this poem in a similar style. Do they believe the excuses? Did similar strange things happen to them that day? Or do they know the real reason that the narrator of the poem was late? It may be useful to do this activity as a class or to split the class into groups. You could use these alternative opening lines as a starting point: 'I don't believe a word that you say, I know the real reason you were late today...'.

• Ask children to write a story about some unusual events during their journey to school. What happened that was unusual? Did it make them late? What happened when they arrived at school? Did their friends believe them or not?

• In groups of four, assign each pupil a verse of the poem and challenge them to learn it by heart. Ask each group to recite the poem to the class. Encourage them to think about clear pronunciation and the importance of reciting at a pace that is easy for the rest of the class to follow.

• Ask pupils to create a comic strip about the journey in the poem. Encourage them to think of a short, concise caption for each picture.

Horrid Henry Tricks the Tooth Fairy

Question Book:
Year 3 Ready, pages 22-23

Author / Source:
Francesca Simon

Genre:
Fiction — novel extract

Cross-curricular links:
*   PSHE (being considerate)
*   Science (looking after teeth)
*   Maths (bar charts)

Introduction

Francesca Simon is an American children's author who has written twenty four books in the popular Horrid Henry series. The series has also been animated for television. Henry is a naughty young boy who is always in trouble — usually for doing something horrible to his brother, Perfect Peter. In this extract, Henry is furious because he is the only child in his class yet to lose any teeth. Start the activity by asking whether anyone in the class has lost a tooth. What did they do with the tooth after it fell out?

Answers

1. three

2. Clare — brainy
    Ralph — impolite
    Margaret — grumpy

3. E.g. swaggered OR showing off

4. E.g. No, because he tries to hide from him and tells him to go away.

5. A tooth.

6. Any appropriate answer. E.g. He will be really angry because Peter has lost a tooth and he hasn't.

Extra Activities

*   Discuss the title of the story with the class. Do pupils think Horrid Henry would be able to trick the tooth fairy or not? Ask pupils to write an ending to the story. What is Henry's plan to trick the tooth fairy? Does it work? What happens in the end?

*   With the whole class, look at the names of the children in the extract. Can pupils think of any adjectives to describe themselves that start with the same letter as their own name?

*   Ask pupils to look at how Henry treats Peter. Is he nice to him? How would they feel if someone treated them like that? Ask them to write down two ways in which Henry could be nicer to Peter.

*   Ask pupils to draw a picture of the tooth fairy. How do they know what she looks like? Ask them to write a paragraph explaining what happens when she comes.

*   Talk to the class about looking after their teeth. How many times a day should they brush their teeth? Do they know which foods are bad for teeth? Write down suggestions on the board into the categories of good/bad for teeth. Ask pupils to create a poster to persuade primary school children to take good care of their teeth. They should include advice about how long to brush your teeth for each day, information on foods that contain a lot of sugar and why they shouldn't be eaten too often, and suggestions of foods that will help your teeth to grow strong and healthy.

*   As a class, conduct a survey of how many teeth pupils have lost. Record the results in a tally chart on the board. Ask pupils to create a bar chart using the information.

Incredible Insects

Question Book:
Year 3 Ready, pages 24-25

Author / Source:
Zoe Fenwick

Genre:
Non-fiction — reference text

Cross-curricular links:
* Geography (Antarctica)
* Science (animal classification)

Introduction

This text introduces pupils to extraordinary insects from all over the world, ranging from a tiny bug just a quarter of a millimetre long to a beetle heavier than a house sparrow. It also gives pupils an opportunity to think about some of the common layout features of non-fiction texts and their effect on the reader. Before reading the text with the class, ask pupils to think of bugs that they have seen outside in the playground or garden and write a list on the board.

Answers

1. Any two from: huge; giant; enormous.

2. Belgica antarctica — can survive its insides freezing
   Horned dung beetle — is the world's strongest insect
   Tinkerbella nana — was discovered in 2013

3. Borneo

4. E.g. Because the places where they live have been destroyed.

5. Any one from: Freezing temperatures; Huge colonies; Recent discoveries; Endangered giants; Long and thin; Super strength.

6. Any appropriate answer. E.g. Belgica antarctica because it can survive in really cold temperatures even when its insides freeze.

Extra Activities

* Ask the class whether this text is a piece of fiction or non-fiction. How can they tell? Ask them to label the layout features of the text (e.g. heading, subheading, photograph) and then discuss the purpose of the different features they have labelled. Can pupils think of any other common features of non-fiction books (e.g. diagrams, an index)? Ask pupils to find these features in books from the school library.

* Ask pupils to pick one of the bugs written on the board in the starter activity and do some research about it. You could give them some bullet points to focus their research (e.g. size, number of legs, habitat, diet). Ask pupils to write a paragraph describing their bug and draw a labelled diagram of it.

* Ask pupils what they know about Antarctica. As a class, find Antarctica on a map and discuss some of the difficulties of surviving in such a cold place. Split the class into groups and assign each group a topic to research (e.g. penguins, South Pole exploration, the effects of climate change). Ask each group to share their findings with the rest of the class.

* Explain the characteristics of insects to the class (e.g. six legs, three main body parts, antennae). Show pupils pictures of some common bugs. Ask pupils to work out whether or not they are insects and explain their reasoning.

Insects	Not insects
bees	worms
butterflies	slugs
ants	spiders
ladybirds	millipedes

Charlie and the Chocolate Factory

Question Book:
Year 3 Ready, pages 26-27

Author / Source:
Roald Dahl
Adapted by Richard George

Genre:
Fiction — playscript

Cross-curricular links:
*   Drama (performance)
*   D&T (set design; product design)
*   Geography (giving directions)

Introduction

Roald Dahl wrote numerous children's stories throughout his life, many of which have been adapted for film and the stage. His famous *Charlie and the Chocolate Factory* was inspired by his experiences of chocolate tasting while at school. It follows a young boy called Charlie who wins a golden ticket for a tour of Willy Wonka's extraordinary factory. This extract introduces children to the format of playscripts. Before reading the text with the class, it may be helpful to discuss the layout of the text and explain various elements, such as lines and stage directions.

Answers

1. E.g. To show that the characters shout a lot.

2. E.g. To show that the names aren't meant to be read out. They're there to tell the actors which are their lines.

3. E.g. Augustus falls into something and then gets sucked up into a pipe. The pipe goes to the Fudge Room.

4. E.g. Worried, because she doesn't know where he has gone or what will happen to him.

5. big

6. E.g. Because the fudge would taste horrible and no-one would buy it.

7. Any appropriate answer. E.g. No, because he doesn't seem very nice. He doesn't care when somebody is in trouble. OR E.g. Yes, because he is funny and I would like to see inside his factory.

Extra Activities

*   Ask students to write a news report describing the events in the extract. Encourage them to think of a headline that sums up the article.

*   Split the class into groups of three and give pupils in each group the roles of Willy Wonka, Mrs Gloop and Augustus. Ask pupils to take turns interviewing each other about what happened at the factory. Encourage pupils to stay in character as they explore how each character feels about the factory tour.

*   Split the class into groups of five and ask them to prepare a performance of the extract. Allow each group to perform for the class, then discuss what was effective in each performance. Encourage the class to think about how an actor's performance can change the effect of their lines.

*   Ask pupils to draw and label a set design for the extract. Encourage them to think about what will need to be included in the set — e.g. a pipe for Augustus to disappear into.

*   As a class, imagine the chocolate factory. How many rooms does it have and what do they contain? Ask pupils to draw a map of the factory, including the Fudge Room mentioned in the extract. They could then use their maps to write directions for Mrs Gloop, telling her how to get to the Fudge Room.

*   Ask pupils to invent a brand new sweet. What is special about it? What does it taste like? What is it made of? Ask them to draw and label their product and design some packaging for it.

The World's Worst Zoo

Question Book:
Year 3 Ready, pages 28-29

Author / Source:
www.metro.co.uk

Genre:
Non-fiction — news article

Cross-curricular links:
- PSHE (honesty)
- Geography (China)

Introduction

After experiencing financial difficulties that left it unable to afford exotic animals for its exhibits, the People's Park Zoo in Luohe, China was forced to find a creative solution. Substituting dogs for lions and rats for snakes, the zoo made headlines around the world for its brazen dishonesty. Before reading the article with the class, ask pupils to discuss the questions in the Pupil Book introduction with a partner.

Answers

1. a news article

2. E.g. To make it stand out from the rest of the text.

3. E.g. Because it lied about what animals it had. It pretended to have lions and snakes, but they were really dogs and rats.

4. E.g. got into trouble

5. foxes

6. E.g. I think that she felt angry and disappointed. She wanted to teach her son about different animals noises, but they only heard barking.

7. Any appropriate answer. E.g. No, because if I went to a zoo I would really like to see a lion. I would be upset if I went to a zoo and just saw a dog instead.

Extra Activities

- Discuss pupils' answers to question 6. Ask pupils to think about whether it was right or wrong for the zoo to try and trick its customers. Do they think honesty is important?

- Ask pupils to imagine they have visited the zoo in the article and get them to write a review of it. Pupils should give the zoo a rating out of 5 and explain why they have awarded that score.

- Ask pupils to plan a story about an animal that escapes from a zoo. Encourage them to start by making a bullet point list of their ideas, and to think carefully about creating a clear beginning, middle and end.

- As a class, imagine the world's best zoo. What would it be like? What animals would it house? Would there be any other attractions? Write down pupils' suggestions on the board. Ask pupils to use this information to create a visitors' guide to the zoo.

- Ask pupils to identify China on a map. Do they know of any animals that are native to China? Divide the class into small groups and assign each group an animal to research (e.g. panda, tiger, snow leopard). Ask them to make a fact sheet about their animal — they should include what it eats, the type of habitat it lives in and some other interesting facts about it. Pupils could also include a drawing of their animal.

Alice's Adventures in Wonderland

Question Book:
Year 3 Ready, pages 30-31

Author / Source:
Lewis Carroll

Genre:
Classic fiction — novel extract

Cross-curricular links:
• Art (drawing)

Introduction

Written by Charles Dodgson under the pen name Lewis Carroll in 1865, *Alice's Adventures in Wonderland* has inspired many works, from art to poetry. It has also been adapted into various films, most famously by both Disney® and Tim Burton. The story follows the adventures of a young girl called Alice who falls down a rabbit hole into the mysterious world of Wonderland. This extract describes Alice's encounter with a group of gardeners who work for the Queen of Hearts. Like all members of the Queen's court, the gardeners are playing cards. Before reading the extract with the class, it may be helpful to explain that some of the characters have numbers for names because they are playing cards.

Answers

1. Seven

2. E.g. Because it shows that Seven is really angry. "Put down" might be used when someone is calm.

3. timidly

4. E.g. Because the Queen wanted red roses and they accidentally planted a white rose tree.

5. right away

6. E.g. Because they are scared of the Queen.

7. Any appropriate answer. E.g. No, because you wouldn't really paint roses if they were the wrong colour.

Extra Activities

• Give pupils four different coloured pens and assign a colour to the characters of Alice, Seven, Five and Two. Ask pupils to re-read the extract, underlining each character's lines with the correct colour. Give each part to a pupil, and read the extract as a class, with a fifth pupil acting as the narrator.

• Ask pupils to rewrite the story in five sentences. Each sentence should answer one of these five questions — where (is it happening?), who (is there?), what (is going on?), why (are they doing it?), who (arrives at the end?).

• Ask pupils to write three bullet points explaining what they think will happen when the Queen arrives. Ask them to compare their points with a partner and discuss how similar or different their ideas are.

• Ask the students to think about the character of the Queen of Hearts. What can they learn about her from this extract? As a class, imagine what she might look like and why people are scared of her. Ask pupils to write a description and then draw a picture.

• As a class, discuss pupils' answers to question 7 in the Question Book and encourage them to think about what makes Wonderland unusual. Get pupils to imagine that they have discovered a magical world. How did they find it? What is it like? Ask them to write a diary entry about their experiences in this magical world, describing the unusual things that happened to them there.

Pupil Progress Chart — Year 1

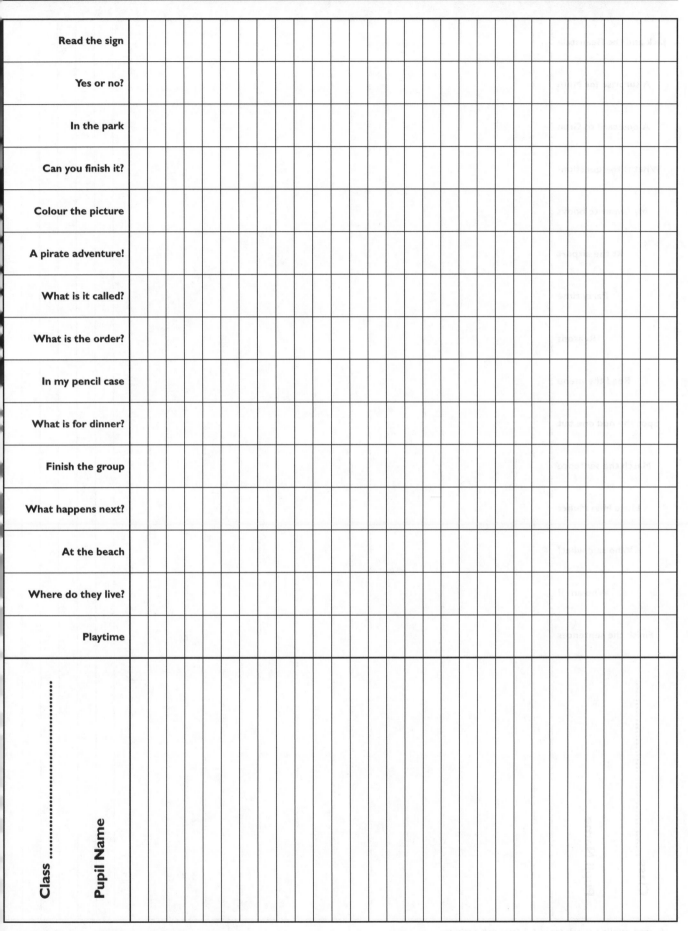

Read the sign																																										
Yes or no?																																										
In the park																																										
Can you finish it?																																										
Colour the picture																																										
A pirate adventure!																																										
What is it called?																																										
What is the order?																																										
In my pencil case																																										
What is for dinner?																																										
Finish the group																																										
What happens next?																																										
At the beach																																										
Where do they live?																																										
Playtime																																										

Class ....

Pupil Name

Award pupils a mark from 1-3 for each activity:

| 1 | = needed a lot of assistance | 2 | = required little assistance | 3 | = completed the activity independently |

Pupil Progress Chart — Year 1

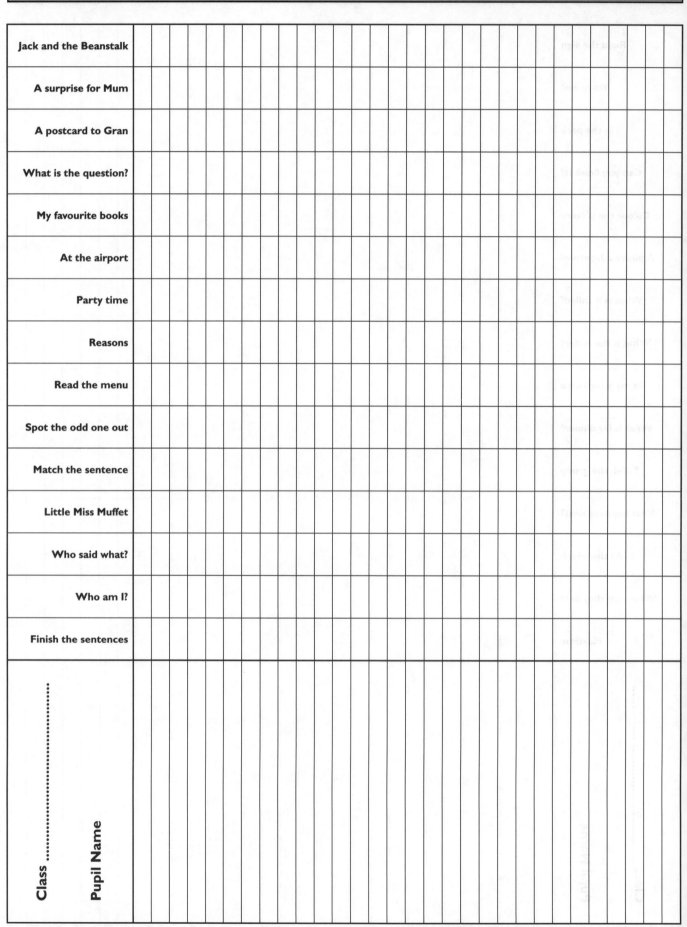

Jack and the Beanstalk																										
A surprise for Mum																										
A postcard to Gran																										
What is the question?																										
My favourite books																										
At the airport																										
Party time																										
Reasons																										
Read the menu																										
Spot the odd one out																										
Match the sentence																										
Little Miss Muffet																										
Who said what?																										
Who am I?																										
Finish the sentences																										
Class .... **Pupil Name**																										

Award pupils a mark from 1-3 for each activity:

| 1 | = needed a lot of assistance | 2 | = required little assistance | 3 | = completed the activity independently |

Pupil Progress Chart — Year 2

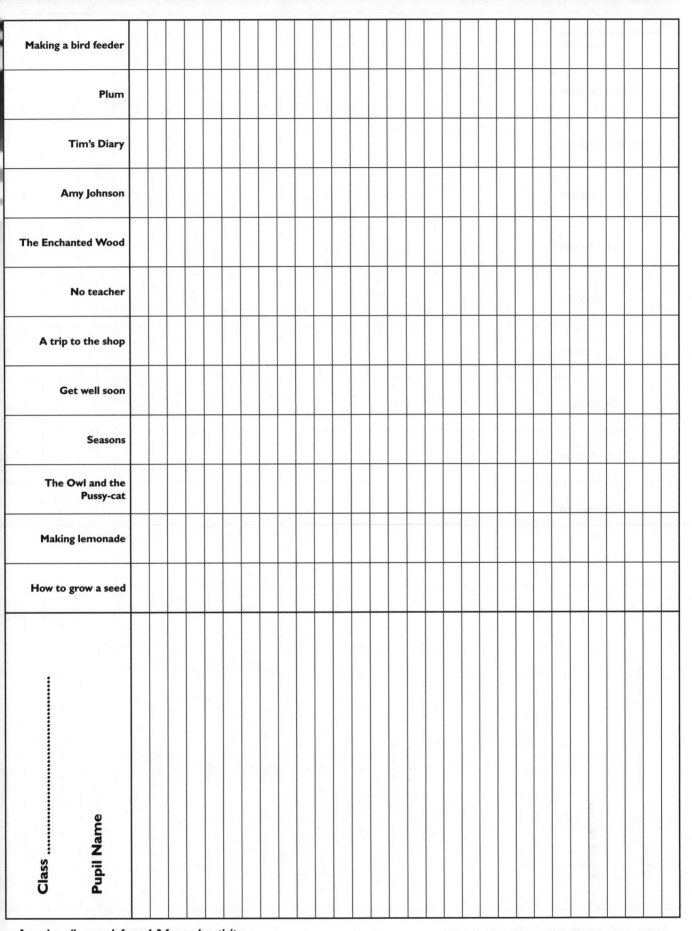

Making a bird feeder																										
Plum																										
Tim's Diary																										
Amy Johnson																										
The Enchanted Wood																										
No teacher																										
A trip to the shop																										
Get well soon																										
Seasons																										
The Owl and the Pussy-cat																										
Making lemonade																										
How to grow a seed																										

Class ....

Pupil Name

Award pupils a mark from 1-3 for each activity:

| 1 | = needed a lot of assistance | 2 | = required little assistance | 3 | = completed the activity independently |

Pupil Progress Chart — Year 2

Pupil Name																							
The Monkeys and the Crocodile																							
The Selfish Giant																							
Slippers at school?																							
Animals																							
Flat Stanley																							
Habitats																							
Sports																							
On the farm																							
Our Solar System																							
The United Kingdom																							
The Tear Thief																							

Class ....

Award pupils a mark from 1-3 for each activity:

1	= needed a lot of assistance	2	= required little assistance	3	= completed the activity independently